Memories of
Alexandria

Memories of Alexandria

From a Void to Nothingness

Ricardo Wahby Tapia

authorHOUSE®

AuthorHouse™
1663 Liberty Drive
Bloomington, IN 47403
www.authorhouse.com
Phone: 1-800-839-8640

First published by AuthorHouse   06/14/2011

ISBN: 978-1-4567-8359-4 (sc)
ISBN: 978-1-4567-8360-0 (ebk)

Printed in the United States of America

Any people depicted in stock imagery provided by Thinkstock are models, and such images are being used for illustrative purposes only. Certain stock imagery © Thinkstock.

This book is printed on acid-free paper.

Photographs (enclosed)

1. That Arthur Miller look. Father in the 30s (Cairo)
2. My "tarbooshed" daddy. (Tetuán 1944)
3. Aunt Marisa and friend on top of the world (the Cheops pyramid 1949)
4. Riding high (Cairo 1949)
5. Father and son (Luxor 1951)
6. Mother tending sheep (Luxor 1952)
7. A candid kiddo at nine (Alexandria 1953)
8. Mother in her prime (Madrid 1958)
9. Father in his fifties (Alexandria 1959)
10. At sixteen. Too young to be a soldier (Alexandria 1960)

ACKNOWLEDGEMENTS

I wish to thank my friends Platon and Hélène Alexiades, Viviane Tawil, Chawky and Adel in Montreal, Robert in Paris, Livio Guerra in Rome, Sandro Manzoni in Switzerland, Jean Pierre Tawil in London, and Mahmud Saleh in Ottawa—for their friendship and for reviving with me over the years many happy memories of our common and distant past.

My very special thanks go to my bosom friend Yorgho in Alexandria, to Jennifer in Madrid who helped me with my English and to my son David Wahby for his disinterested technical cooperation.

Quote:

FROM A VOID TO NOTHINGNESS:
From the void we come from to the nothingness we're heading to. What is left is a short spell called illusion.
Ricardo Wahby Tapia.

Glossary

Al Sham: the Levant
Baksheesh: tip.
Batta: ducky.
Bawab: door-keeper.
Betaa el ayal: pederast.
Caracol: police station
Effendi: sir.
Emshe: go away.
Falafel: fried balls made of fava beans.
Farrash: caretaker, janitor
Fedan: acre
Fellaheen: peasants.
Fool: cooked brown beans.
Frangi/a: European.
Galabiya: man's robe wore in the street or at home.
Gamoosa: Egyptian water-buffalo.
Gawafa: guava
Ghoul: Arab demon.
Guarb: west.
Habibi: my love (also dear or darling)
Hadj: pilgrim to Mecca.
Halawa: hair remover; also Egyptian sweet.
Homos: sort of salad
Horreya: Liberty/freedom.
Kaput: condoms
Khamseen: spring wind
Kharchuf: artichoke.
Khawal: faggot.
Khawagat: Egyptians of foreign descent and foreigners.
Kuayes: fine
Leb: sunflower seeds.

Measal: Arab water pipe tobacco.
Makwagi: ironer
Misr: Egypt.
Mokhabarat: State security; Egyptian secret services.
Nahas: copper
Nasr: victory
Pasha & Bey: Turkish titles used today as a sign of respect.
Raïs: leader and President.
Samna: fat used for cooking.
Shaweesh: policeman
Sheesha: Arab water-pipe.
Shorta: policeman, police station.
Sorsar: cockroach.
Suffragi: footman.
Tarboosh: hat of Turkish origin.
Taffi el nur: switch off the lights.
Targama: translation.
Umm: mother
Zabet: army officer.

INTRODUCTION

I was busy writing this book when, at the end of January, 2011, all hell broke loose in Egypt in the shape of a general uprising that took to the streets of Cairo and other major cities in a massive protest against injustice, corruption, poverty, tyranny, persecution and lack of freedom which finally provoked the downfall of President Mohamed Hosni Mubarak.

This was the second "white revolution" Egypt had witnessed in the last sixty years. The first, in July 1952, was a military coup that brought down the monarchy to install a dictatorial republic which had lasted to this day.

To the eyes of the world, Egypt was a safe, stable country, contented and submissive, which had had only three presidents in the last six decades. Since 1981, the country had been harshly ruled by President Mubarak, an absolute but accommodating dictator in his eighties, who was humorously known by the witty Egyptian people as "Mubarak the first" or the "last pharaoh". In his inexhaustible lust for power and fortune and to keep the people under the ominous thumb of his family, he had foreseen a family dynasty in which his son Gamal Mubarak would take up, the reins of the country after his demise.

Like a premonition I visited Alexandria in November 2010, just two months before the uprising, to revive old memories and gather new information. I witnessed during my conversations with the man in the street, the discontent, distrust, despair and weariness of the poor and middle classes.

But this book is not about Egypt's recent "people's revolution", its present situation, troubles and misfortunes; neither is it an outlook on its possible future, which will always look bleak and hopeless to me and for reasons other than those which caused the massive protest.

It's about the up-rooted *khawagat* (Egyptian foreigners) who, many decades ago, were my classmates and my friends when Egypt was a very different and a much more agreeable place to live in. It's also the story of people from different cultures and backgrounds caught up in the hectic history of Spain and Egypt, amidst the turmoil of wars, revolution and oppression from the late thirties to the early sixties.

In spite of the recent events in other Arab countries which are shaking the whole of the Middle East, I haven't changed a word of what I initially intended to express when I started, more than a year ago to write these memoirs of my early years. They are a true and surrealistic account of bygone times and a philosophical and cynical approach of what the present and the future have to offer.

MEMORIES OF ALEXANDRIA

(From a Void to nothingness)

A philosophical surrealistic story of
bygone times

CHAPTER ONE

I was almost twenty years old when on 14th April, 1964 I left Egypt on a one-way ticket to Spain. Early in the afternoon, I boarded the *Benidorm* which cast off that same evening, arriving ten days later at the Spanish city of Valencia, after two stopovers at the ports of Beirut in Lebanon and Latakia in Syria.

On the morning of my departure, and with plenty of time to spare, a friend of the family drove me and my parents to the Port of Alexandria. My best friend and bosom buddy Yorgho (Greek for George) followed us on the blue Bianchi racing bicycle which I had given him the night before as a parting gift.

Although he pedalled hard to keep up with our speeding car, he was soon left behind when our vehicle accelerated on a long avenue leading to the waterfront and the harbour; he then stopped his bicycle, stood there for a moment and turned back towards home. He knew we would not see each other for a very long time, maybe never again, and he had tried by this senseless pursuit to delay our final separation for as long as he could.

The freighter *Benidorm* and three other almost identical vessels were the property of Naviera Exportadora Agricola, a shipping company whose Head Office was in Princesa Street in Madrid. It was specialised in the conveyance of agricultural products and brought to Alexandria the tins of Spanish virgin olive oil my mother used for cooking. We knew those ships well, as we had travelled on them in 1957 and 1958 when, after the 1956 Suez war, Mom and I left Egypt to spend a year in Spain.

Each of those freighters called "mixed-cargos" was equipped with eight double cabins and in the summertime, it was a relaxing delight for holidaymakers, to embark for a round trip which could last up to twenty days, depending on scheduled and unscheduled stopovers, should the Captain receive an urgent radio message from his Madrid Headquarters ordering him to change his course to pick-up some last minute freight at a Mediterranean harbour.

The customary one or two day stopovers included ports like Marseilles, Genoa, Piraeus and Malta, which made these casual cruises very attractive; it was like living in a comfortable, clean guest house, while visiting at random the most important Mediterranean cities. These sea trips were the quiet and pleasant forerunners of today's hectic cruises, (or cattle boats) which pack by the thousands a tutti-frutti of nationalities, and are devised for the bored, hollow masses which pay good money to overfill their plates and be constantly entertained.

Back then, vacations meant relaxation, total independence and a taste of the good life. The passengers took their meals in the Officers' mess with the Captain presiding and the atmosphere was always gleeful and relaxed.

The main freight from Spain to Alexandria was onions and potatoes; the return cargo was fine Egyptian long fibre cotton for the Spanish mills and clothing factories.

It was late on the evening of April 24th, when we docked in Valencia. My mother's sister, Marisa then in her early forties, and her lifelong partner Julian in his late fifties, were standing on the wharf waiting for me. As the ship was towed sideways towards the dock, I stood on the deck and watched them, smiling and waving and talking, as if they had stood their whole life there, waiting for the arrival of their prodigal nephew.

My aunt Marisa was my mother's unmarried sister and I was her one and only and favourite nephew. I slept on board that night, and early next morning, as soon as I cleared Passport Control and Customs, we drove the three hundred and fifty kilometres to Madrid in my aunt's Seat 600 car, (the Spanish version of the Fiat 600) arriving in the evening after a stopover for lunch.

The year before, in June 1963, I had finished high school (*the Baccalauréat*) at the Lycée Français in Alexandria, and it was agreed with my parents, that my aunt would take good care of me and provide for my needs while I decided what I wanted to do with my life—which could easily go to waste, as I felt uneasy about attending University, and neither was I very enthusiastic about starting to look for a job.

My first impressions of Madrid made me feel as if I had taken a one-way ticket to the blues. It was hot for April, even by local standards, and though I had been brought up in the warm climate of Egypt, I disliked just like my father did, the heat and the brutal sun. Madrid is an artificially watered oasis in the middle of the Castilian steppe.

The heat and the drought and the cloudless and desolate white-blue skies linger day in day out, week after week and month after month from April or May, to sometimes late October. Springs and early autumns were like summers, summers were like hell and winters were like shit and could be mild or cold but always dry and polluted by traffic fumes, small-time factories and out-dated coal heating systems.

I didn't expect my newfound surroundings to be "fresh and green like merry England", as I had often seen in British films, but I had anticipated something different, maybe a more "European" environment as if I knew what the word "European" meant.

What I had surely forgotten was what Spain was like during the late fifties, when my mother and I had spent a full year in Madrid. Or maybe my inclinations and priorities had changed during those last six years when I shifted from boy to young man.

The climate, but most of all, the cultural environment so alien to my own, made me wish I had landed somewhere else. In those early days, I often thought of the French who said that "Africa begins at the Pyrenees", though they meant it, not only for geographical causes, but for political reasons as well.

The French writer and philosopher André Gide also wrote that "nothing discourages more the mind or the ability to think than blue skies".

If one thinks metaphorically, of the position of the human brain in geographical terms, meaning by that the ability to think productively equated with earth latitudes, one will observe that in very warm climates, where full moon and starry skies are unique, of incomparable beauty, the brain is located down under, between the legs and sex is men's basic issue. In temperate Mediterranean Latin countries, the brain is placed in the stomach: good eating, talking about dinner while having lunch and discussing food all the time are the main concerns. Finally, in countries were the sun is scarce the brain is located where it should be, up in the skull, facilitating sensible productive thinking.

After millions of years of evolution, man still behaves in many ways like the primate he sprang from: thinking is not his cup of tea. Intelligence and creativity still rest in the brains of a privileged few, who are fathering all inventions and discoveries and pushing the machine of civilisation to dangerous and unpredictable limits.

Anyway, thinking is now out of fashion and is barely practised anymore. It is the target of the nefarious, global society, supported by a disrespectful, unchained and frenzied media, whose aim is to numb the masses, encouraging a useless, destructive consumption and raising generation after generation of mediocre, illiterate, weaklings and unimaginative simpletons.

I have always loved my "bred-in" English and French languages and cultures, as if my father had been British and my mother French or vice-versa. Thus, Spain became for me like the dark side of the moon. I had no friends with whom I could share my cosmopolitan background or the languages I longed to speak; mother sent me from Alexandria the movie magazines I hungered for, but were impossible to find in Madrid. Radio stations broadcast idiotic programmes and the two available television channels, transmitted rubbish, such as football matches, (in Egypt, football was considered as the sport for the rabble who filled the stadiums and was not in the least appreciated by the prosperous classes who watched and practised more sophisticated sports such as basket-ball or tennis), bullfighting, moronic shows, old Spanish films, stupid American series and other cheap stuff for the benefit of nincompoops.

Nothing has changed much, either in Spain or worldwide, except that massive-media-indoctrinated-audiences have multiplied the factor of idiocy and mediocrity ad infinitum.

That "hopeless Spanish situation" didn't help much to enhance or improve my intellect, but rather encouraged my shyness and apathy, increased my built-in sense of inactivity and lack of determination. Considering my lack of purpose and my staggeringly weak will-power, these negative aspects of the country I was just discovering were far from presenting me with the incentive needed to start a creative and productive life.

I stopped going to the movies as the films just like the American series shown on television were dubbed into Spanish. The American and French and Italian actors, all had the same monotonous voice, as the number of persons who were dubbing the foreign actors amounted to a couple of dozens of unprofessional voices, most of them speakers from the radio, the television and the commercials.

The first "massacred" film I watched was *The Pink Panther* and I acquired, then and there, such a profound disgust for the cinema, (which had always been my hobby and my solace) that I hardly set foot in a movie house again, until many years later when certain cinemas started to show subtitled films in their original version.

I felt surrounded by meek and conceited, (a difficult but possible combination) sexually frustrated men with brilliantined hair and pencil moustaches, wearing dark suits and colourless ties even in the middle of the blazing summers, and by sex-starved-tight-cunt-half-virgin frustrated females that roamed dance halls and parties searching for some light romance and marriage, who vehemently refused to go all the way. A fresh, candid piece of pussy was out of reach. In dance halls and parties, women proved their virtue and impenetrability by squeezing their thighs and repelling close belly contact while dancing a "slow". With forearms and fists, they pushed back the sexual advances of their partners, who were trying, with all their might, to pull them in, closer and closer to their scrotums. To the observers those dance floors looked like a weird slow-motion wrestling math.

All that, was unexpected for an immature and carefree dickhead like me, who didn't know then as he never learned later, which way he was heading, or what he expected or wanted from life.

Swinging London was still unheard of and the Beatles were considered by the local "establishment" who favoured the deafening Arab-tainted and pathetic flamenco music, as a quartet of untalented, noisy, guitar-scratchers and hairy-hoodlums. In those days, long hair was a major and sickly obsessive issue, considered by most of the populace, as the disgusting privilege of foreign faggots and hippies. Traditional Spanish values encouraged and widely publicised by the Regime propaganda machine, made of Spain "the upholder of eternal, moral western values", whatever those values might have been. I was appalled by one of the many idiotic questions the Beatles were asked, after their first and only concert in the Madrid bullfighting arena, by one moronic journalist who found nothing better to say than: "Hey Beatles, when are you going to cut your hair?" Looking back, I concur that those impressions I felt as a new-comer, were unsympathetic and harsh, but I must admit, that back then, I didn't mind much. I liked what I saw in Spain and I tried to melt into that newfound society. I was content to enjoy my new freedom and the easy way of life that was opening to me.

To succeed amongst one's "peers" one has to be a moron, or make believe you are; if one doesn't graze their same fodder, one will be considered a weirdo because of one's differences with the rest of the fold.

If I had felt and knew then what I feel and know now, my life would have been . . . . well, I guess the same, as there is no escape from oneself.

I had just run away from a hard Egyptian dictatorship to Franco's milder paternalistic Regime (my personal point of view) which allowed quite a lot of leeway if one didn't meddle in leftist political activities or better still, in no political activities at all (Franco knew best). I didn't mind that, as I thought then, as I think now, that politics are the lowest possible occupation and a nasty habit, only fit for unscrupulous roaches. I loathe rotten politicians of all shapes and colours from the left and from the right and from all the corners of the earth, as much as I despise their counterpart, the political press which bullies its way around through deception and lies. Both "powers" portray the perfect pillars of corruption, deceit and hypocrisy and, like thirsty, unquenchable leeches, survive and thrive feeding on each other's blood.

Spain was not a democracy by any stretch of the imagination, but it provided certain advantages and perfectly suited my contradictory and unsettled personality. I reckoned that tobacco and booze were cheap, streets were safe at night, people were inefficient but nice, stress was unknown, and the advance guard of what was to become the tourist invasion of the sixties, was already in town and at the seaside resorts.

Opportunities for a good fuck were abundant. There were plenty of visiting females on the streets, in the cafeterias and in the Prado Museum, (which I used as a hunting ground) with guidebooks in hand, staring in awe at the Masters' paintings. They were easy prey and if one knew how to handle them, they were always willing and ready for a one-night stand. My fluency in English and French gave me a definitive edge over my Spanish "competitors" whose faces spoke of a sexual hunger, that led to impatience, bad manners and sometimes aggressiveness when their awkward advances were refused by the reluctant victims, while their restrained desire glowed in their dark eyes like two small, twinkling dicks.

For years, I have kept blaming myself (and I still do) for living in a country so incompatible with my culture and my background. All through my adult years, because of my knowledge of languages and my looks, I have been fortunate to work for International Corporations and I have had opportunities I ignored to leave and settle in other countries as a man of substance. But I never had the guts to call it quits and to leave for better or maybe for worse. Maybe it's because I had already learned that discontent, frustration and unhappiness are deeply and permanently anchored within oneself and that no matter where one might go, new surroundings and different cultures will never alter that inner desperate condition.

The expression "the choices we make dictate the life we lead" is not totally true as there is no escape from oneself. The fact of being unable to change one's life or the chain of events life is all about is called fate and fate is mostly hereditary because that's what fate's all about: a pattern imbibed in one's brain through inherited genes, which makes it impossible to follow the paths intelligence and imagination suggest.

It's easy to reach to the skies for an idea, but to bring it down to earth and to put it into practice is a different matter. The French expression "il n´est pas bien dans sa peau" (he is not comfortable in his skin) also meaning "he doesn't like what he is or what he stands for" is very illuminating in the sense that the weight one carries inside is hard to bear, but impossible to shed. If we add to this erratic but true equation the factor "unexpected", the final verdict on man's destiny is precise, unmovable and already regulated like clockwork.

I didn't have the courage to trust my guts. No one is to blame; I was coy and lazy and I carved my fate. All things considered, I think I have been lucky to have survived and sometimes thrived for all those years in a milieu which I didn't like, toiling in boring jobs for which I felt no interest or passion.

CHAPTER TWO

When I left Egypt in 1964, I was angered and bitter; the good memories of my childhood had vanished or were frozen deep inside me. The Egyptian *Khawagat* (foreigners born in Egypt) who were being deprived of their assets by the 1952 revolution and its aftermath were still leaving the country en masse. Their legacy of buildings and imposing villas had started their definitive decay and Alexandria was slowly becoming an Arab borough.

During my final months there, I felt a prisoner of a dictatorship which had deprived Egyptians from the most elementary of all liberties: the right to move freely and to leave at will. An exit visa was then necessary to depart the country and the only way to get it, was to produce a contract issued by a foreign Company that vouched for a steady job abroad. Another possible option for Egyptians was to emigrate to North America or Australia, but the authorities could naively or angrily ask the would-be emigrant, how anyone in his sound mind could ever want to leave Egypt, that paradise on earth, to live a hell in distant, sinful, soulless countries.

My aunt in Madrid sent me a fake work contract, but it took my father and me seven months of nerve-breaking red tape before my exit visa was stamped on my passport and I was finally authorised to leave the country.

During those months of fear and incertitude, my dislike for Egypt increased. I even regarded the familiar open sea as a hostile barrier that kept me locked in a country I wanted no more and where I didn't belong. I gazed at the horizon and imagined the free shores of Europe on the other side of the divide.

I reckon that the government carried out this drastic method to keep the people in and to avoid a mass exodus of discontented and out-of-work Egyptians, who would have left the country to flood Europe. There they would hang on to menial jobs, hustling, begging or stealing, and face deportation just as blacks, North Africans and East Europeans are now doing. The situation in Europe was somewhat different fifty years ago. Unwanted immigration was not tolerated and laws on this matter were strongly enforced. Illegal immigrants were kept at bay and not so easily accepted as they are to-day.

President Nasser was also probably dismayed by the loss of "Egyptian brain power" concerning those highly-regarded professionals, who could make a better living anywhere in the world. (Years later, the doors opened and millions of Egyptians from all walks of life left Egypt to work in America, Europe and the Gulf States).

But Nasser or the *Raïs* (the leader) could not take the risk of letting his "scum of the earth" tarnish abroad the image of his 1952 white revolution. He also aspired to be the champion of an unlikely united Arab world and the leader of non aligned countries like Indonesia and Yugoslavia, respectively teaming-up with his political "neutral" buddies President Sukarno and Marshall Tito.

I realise that my small temporary inconvenience of feeling a prisoner was unimportant compared to the hardship of those who during the ill-fated post-revolution years had been nationalised (robbed) and lost everything to the State, including lands, real estate, businesses, factories and personal wealth; or of those innocent Jews who, for no apparent reason, were imprisoned for months at the start of the six-day war in June 1967 in the Cairo prison of Abu Zaabal.

I felt very strongly against Egypt and its totalitarian Regime, and when I arrived in Spain, I tried to erase, or at least cover-up as well as I could, all traces of my Egyptian past. I told inquisitors that I had a foreign accent because I had lived abroad for many years, and that my unusual surname (Wahby), was, although I wasn't too sure, anything from Turkish to Anglo Saxon to Irish to German, as it had all the necessary ingredients including a W and a Y with an H in the middle.

My friend Sandro who has lived in Switzerland since 1956, but who was born in Alexandria and remained there longer than I did, told me once that when we left Egypt under those unusual and unsavoury circumstances, it was like a *khazuk* which took a long time to digest.

The *khazuk* was a well-known Turkish torture and execution method which consisted of sitting the naked convict on a sharp, well greased strong wooden spike that slowly pierced his anus into his rectum and intestines, to finally kill the man when it reached some vital organ. Various old illustrations picture the *khazuk* joyfully springing out of the mouth of a wretched corpse, which is doubtful, because to guarantee the firmness and the stability of the stick, it was never long enough to run right through the body. On the contrary, it was rather short, sixty centimetres at most, and was firmly planted into the ground to avoid any awkward up-rooting during executions.

At times these executions in which the victim was impaled were performed in public in the banqueting hall to provide guests with some light entertainment during

State celebrations. One sensitive guest was so upset by the gruelling ceremony that he puked all over the place, spoilt everyone's appetite and made a fool of himself. He was immediately removed by the guards and impaled next to the previous victim—for disturbing the peace.

However, the Rumanian *khazuk* (Rumania was for sometime a Turkish Province) was as long as a lance and could pierce the body from bottom to top.

The word is still widely used in Arab countries today to describe something nasty that befalls one and can be translated as "a pain in the arse" which carries a surprising similarity to the Turkish origin of the word.

The *khazuk* which took more than thirty years to digest was the grudge I held against a regime that was not only wrecking the economy of the country, but ruining and expelling hundred of thousands of foreigners, and keeping me in, when all I wanted was to get out.

I cannot say that I cared for the events that were dramatically changing Egypt. I wasn't worried about the day-to-day deteriorating situation, or of things going from bad to worse. Unlike other Egyptian-foreigners, I never loved Egypt. Moreover my folks had no wealth to lose to the new order, and I always knew, much before those events took place, that my future was not in Egypt, but elsewhere. But I was childishly angry at everything and everyone because I wanted to beat it, to leave forever, and as an Egyptian, I wasn't allowed to. Egypt had become a heinous magnet, my "personal *khazuk*", which kept driving in, when all I wanted was to break free and leave forever.

Nothing has changed much in Egypt in the last sixty years; corruption still runs high. The nouveaux riches are richer than their predecessors ever were and openly parade their wealth and status while the millions of poor grow poorer and show no sign of hope or improvement. Finally and most importantly, the rampant birth rate and general discontent will undoubtedly bring the country down, leaving it in the hands of fanatics, who are building their power base, by gaining support from the destitute by feeding them with money and empty promises.

Their takeover of the country could have unforeseen and dramatic consequences not only for Egypt but for the whole Middle East. It may take a decade or more, but the frightening facts are there.

Since I left, forty seven years ago, I have returned three times to Egypt, twice on business, when I was working for the American Express Travel Services in Madrid. I then spent two days in Cairo, with a quick one day escapade to Alexandria to see my lifelong friend Yorgho.

My last trip to Alexandria dates back to November 2010, when I spent five full days with Yorgho and his wife Lody revisiting the town. I call it the "reconciliation trip", and gave me what was probably my final outlook on a world that was once ours, but which has slowly slipped away and gone astray.

I walked again, up and down the neighbourhood alleys I knew so well, now hardly recognisable and which no longer remembered the footsteps of our lost past.

The streets look narrower and dirtier; they're smelly and filled with sombre faces I don't recall or recognise, while monotonous loudspeakers on street corners constantly remind the faithful of their daily prayers.

Nothing remains of the time when many others like me, now scattered all over the world trod these same streets, eating and shopping, enjoying and living the present, still unconcerned for the future which looked improbable and very remote.

I now think of another Greek also named Yorgho, I met last November, who is a close friend of my Yorgho. He looks like the actor Topol and had worked forty years for the NCR (National Cash Register) Corporation in Alexandria. His home, in my former neighbourhood of Camp-César, is on the ground floor of a cracked building, in what was once a pleasant and quiet area. He came to the window to greet us as we passed by. He looked misplaced but unaffected amidst the decline of his surroundings. He had been all through the years, slowly inoculated with the vaccine of deterioration and has thus become immune and oblivious to his decaying environment.

CHAPTER THREE

My father Mohamed Wahby was Egyptian of Caucasian Turkish origin. He was born in 1902, in the small village of Biba, south of Cairo, in the rich agricultural area of Al Fayoum.

His family probably moved to Cairo around 1908. His ancestors had arrived in Egypt from the vast Ottoman Empire in the nineteenth century, during the Mohamed Ali Egyptian dynasty which spanned one hundred and fifty years.

He was tall, with snow white skin, dark green-blue eyes, a receding hairline and an air of premature maturity, which, combined with his patrician manner, made him look older than he was. He had a sad nature and looking back now, I think he was in a constant state of mild depression.

Some people are born with a happy nature, while others are not. Depressions, (without the unbearable anxiety or anguish) were called the blues, or in French *le cafard* (the cockroach), which is a graphic expression, probably meaning that it must be lousy to feel as low as a cockroach. In the old days, depressions were not treated or nursed, as they presently are, by expert psychiatrists who are in the hustling business of plundering the moron's wallets by listening to their crap, to grant uncompromising advice, shrink their brains even further, prescribe all kind of anti-depressive pills, and milk the submissive golden calf as long as possible.

The psychiatrist and the analyst sessions have almost replaced the good old confessions practised in Catholic countries by priests. The person seeking confession would unload the whole weight of his problems and frustrations into a sympathetic ear that was also the ear of God. It was free and enlightening. A priest doesn't charge for his services; he only prescribes a little prayer which is much healthier for the body and the soul than any chemical product on the market.

My father seldom lost his temper. He was introverted, unobtrusive and silent. In public, he displayed a gentle smile to prove that he cared for people and things, but he had no need for company or for the hustle and bustle of social life.

The imbeciles who unfortunately (or fortunately for the smooth running of society) account for a large percentage of mankind think that loneliness and silence equal death. Like herds of cattle, they long to be packed into open spaces such as stadiums and amusement parks, crowded in downtown streets and outdoor cafés enjoying the deafening rumble of traffic in their ears and breathing the sweet smell of pollution deep into their lungs; they love to be squeezed into giant aircrafts bound for exotic destinations and faraway countries they have no business going to, but hope by that, to escape from the mediocrity of their lives and the desolation of their minds.

The new society is the culprit for idiocy, suppressing personality, and confusing the crowds to achieve the required massive consumption by obedience with the wicked television as the spearhead of cretinism. In his wildest dreams, Lenin could never have imagined that such an apparently harmless weapon as television could ever be invented to reduce the rabble to a mindless state.

My father was born into the Muslim faith but soon discarded all religions. He could as well have been born a Christian, Jew or Hindu. Children are like young calves, branded at birth with the hot iron of their parents' faith, and are brainwashed into the falsehood and hypocrisy of the creed. Not many believe but many follow.

Religions represent the summit of stupidity and weakness, which is the stuff, man is made of. If a child has been indoctrinated, it is difficult for him when a rational and practical adult to "completely" reject his religion and abandon the dogmas which he was brought to follow. Something will always tickle inside, in the same way smokers, alcoholics and drug addicts, although cured of their vices, will sometimes feel a certain draw towards their addictions.

My father knew that religions are a "must" invented for the sole purpose of providing the crowd with spiritual solace as well as an anchor, linking individuals to the recognition and social status they crave for, and without which, they would be lost.

It is a fact that without the cementing effect of religion, the masses would lack the basic guiding lines and could easily go astray. The day man is rid of all religions and other similar superstitions (which will never happen), he will be a little less weak and a little less stupid.

My grandfather's name had been Ishag (Arabic for Isaac). He later changed it to Hussein to fit a Muslim environment suspicious of Jewish names. I never met his parents who had died before my arrival in Egypt. I was even unaware of his mother's name and his father's profession.

Recently I was puzzled to read in a book written by exiled Egyptian Jews, that our family name Wahba—ending in a—is a Muslim name as well as a Jewish one. This is confusing and contradictory because both Wahby and Wahba originate from Wahabi, the man who founded the eponymous sect of Muslim puritans, on which Saudi Arabia's laws and rule is based. (Egypt is being contaminated by Wahabi Muslim fundamentalism, imported from Saudi Arabia by Egyptian migrants who have been living and working in the Gulf countries since the seventies).

If my father had Jewish roots, and genes possess the memory of time, the love he felt for Spanish culture and language could be explained and traced back to his possible Sephardic origins.

In the Spain of 1492, the short-sighted Catholic Monarchs (Ferdinand and Isabella) kicked the hell out of the Spanish Jews who had productively lived in the country for many centuries and who were the backbone of the economy. Those Jews (as well as the Spanish Muslims who were also expelled) found shelter in the Ottoman Empire and were welcomed by the wise and broad-minded Sultan of Constantinople, who understood that these newcomers would enrich his vast domains.

The Monarchs, through this brutal deed, impoverished their realm, by draining away its two most important assets: money and culture, respectively in the hands of the Jews and Muslims. The fate of the country was sealed and left in the hands of the Roman Catholic Church and its poor illiterate rabble and it took Spain five hundred years to recover from such brainless agony.

However, not all Jews left Spain. Some managed to stay, easing their way to legality with bribes and voluntary conversion to Catholicism. They became good Catholics—on the surface at least—and some of them, as proof of trust and sincerity in their new convictions, even changed their family names to popular Catholic names such as Santa Maria, Santa Cruz and Santa Marta. I assume, though, that they secretly kept practising their faith they had apparently buried, but which kept burning inside their little bleeding, weeping hearts.

The Egyptian Sephardic Jews—those who came from Syria, Palestine and elsewhere in the Levant—spoke Ladino, which was the old language used in Spain in the middle ages, incomprehensible today, and bearing no resemblance to modern Spanish.

The Jews who stayed in Spain were assimilated over the centuries into Spanish society and today most of them are oblivious of their distant origins. However I can see and sense their original genes, which have survived through the generations, roaming the streets of modern Spain, reflected in their features, complexion and certain traits of character that sometimes make them different quieter and wiser than the rest of the population.

I lacked the curiosity to ask dad about his origins. But how could a boy ask such questions to a disillusioned man well into his fifties.

My father was a civil servant: he worked in government schools and was a teacher of history and geography. Towards the end of his career, he became a headmaster. In the late fifties he was promoted to second class civil servant, which was almost the peak of the teaching hierarchy, and one step short from a first class position, top of the administrative scale. This promotion slightly increased his salary and finally gave him an opportunity, when he was recalled to Alexandria, as headmaster of a secondary boys' school.

I never saw my father displaying the traditional Turkish hat called *tarboosh* although I have seen photographs of him wearing it in the late thirties. The *tarboosh was* brought to Egypt by the Ottomans and has been an Egyptian tradition and institution for many centuries. Its use was compulsory for Government Officials as well as for the Egyptian ruling classes (the Pashas and the Beys) until it was abolished after the 1952 revolution. The *tarboosh*, which looks like an upside down ice bucket, is a round red or blue felt hat with a short and black pony tail on top.

Dad was the youngest of four children. His eldest brother Ali Bey (a Bey is an honorary Turkish title still used as a mark of respect) was fifteen years his senior. He was an officer in the Army and rose to the rank of Brigadier. In his youth, my uncle did service in the Sudan, then an Egyptian colony and a human quarry that supplied the Egyptian army with black soldiers, as well as with cheap labour for Egyptian households, in the form of tall and thin *suffragis* (footmen), strong *bawab* (door keepers) and other types of men-servants.

At the request of his friend Louis Napoleon, Emperor of France, a contingent of black soldiers was sent to Mexico in the nineteenth century by the Khedive Ismail of Egypt to fight for the puppet Emperor Maximilian who had been placed by France on the Mexican throne. It seemed that these blacks were best suited to resist the harsh Mexican climate.

My uncle Ali Bey was a hefty fellow, over six feet tall with a strong character and a will of iron. He proudly sported a bushy white Ottoman moustache which he regularly waxed to keep the tips up in the air like two tiny and inquisitive antennas.

The brothers had two fair-haired blue-eyed single sisters who lived in Alexandria, in a villa by the Corniche (the seaside promenade which stretches for more than fifteen kilometres from one side of the town to the other). I never knew much about my Egyptian aunts and neither was I much aware of their existence, as my mother kept to a civilized and necessary minimum our relations with my father's family. It's a pity because it would have been interesting to know more about the family, especially now that I'm writing about them.

They were good people, of Turkish aristocratic descent, open-minded and talkative and I am sure I could have learned a lot by asking and listening. The problem my mother had to face when we first met them was that we didn't speak Arabic or English which were the only languages they knew. As she felt uncomfortable about the lack of communication, she started to curtail our relations, leaving only the indispensable calls on two annual festivities, one being *Eid al Ahda* (sacrifice day) and the other, *Eid al Fitr,* the end of the fasting month of Ramadan.

My uncle Ali Bey had a son, an army officer, called Fuad and a sexy daughter with great thighs who visited us regularly. In my teens, she became the mental target of my hidden desires and the inspiration for my early fantasies and masturbations, which I performed at home, sitting on the bathroom bidet or, with narcissistic designs, standing up, facing the mirror. We called her "Fifi" and I never knew her real name. She married a bald army officer named Mustapha (military tradition ran in the family) whom I sometimes envied because he had exclusive access to that lavish body of hers, although if I believe my mother's gossip, she cuckolded him all the time with his fellow officers. My cousin Fuad followed his father's footsteps, became an officer and fought as a lieutenant in the May 1948 war with Israel which began the day after we arrived to Egypt.

No one called my father Mohamed. The name didn't become his persona. So it was straight Wahby for my mother and for his friends and Mr Wahby for everyone else. When he first met my mother, he didn't tell her his name was Mohamed. It didn't match his blatantly European physique, but only with the image people in those days (and even today) had of Muslims. So he told her that he his name was Theodore (like Teddy Roosevelt), which in Spanish is a romantic and languid name that can be mispronounced to sound like *te adoro* (I adore you). At times, he had a senseless and strange sense of humour and liked to juggle with words repeating once and again well know phrases and idioms. But maybe, and in spite of his solemn appearance, he also knew a thing or two, and wished to be a reflection of the well-known French poet, writer and critic Théophile Gautier, who loved and visited Egypt. Gauthier also travelled to Spain and wrote about it one century before my father's time.

CHAPTER FOUR

My mother Carmen Tapia was born in Madrid in 1918. She lost her mother at eighteen, during the Spanish civil war. As the eldest, she clashed with her father after my grandmother passed away, for he disregarded and disrespected his two daughters, moving out of the family home and settling someplace else with his mistress.

Like all Spaniards Mom was brought-up in the Catholic faith but she thought that mother church was a pathetic farce, especially after witnessing the cruelty and the killing on both sides during the war. When their villages were taken by the Nationalists, the rightist priests, seeking revenge, would hand Franco's troops a list of those in their community they thought were Republicans or Communist sympathizers. These were immediately executed without a hearing or a trial. The abuses committed by both the Republicans and the Nationalists took a heavy toll, spoiled her character, affected her way of thinking and disillusioned her for the rest of her life.

My folks were straightforward and pragmatic and never cared about religion. No nonsense was the name of our game. God was contemplated within the framework of a reasonable thinking. They didn't think much of the Holy Books which they beheld as dubious and non-proven eastern adventures, spread by an illiterate, ragged, scruffy lot from the old times. Thus, I was neither baptized nor circumcised nor brought up under the banner of any religion. Mom however taught me a short, easy prayer I recited at bedtime. "It's you tiny insurance with God, in case you need him," she said; "If you feel the need to talk to Him, do it directly without the intervention of middlemen. That was good advice and that's what I have selfishly and secretly done in my moments of deep despair.

However in 1971, at twenty-seven, and against my convictions, I hypocritically accepted baptism as a necessary step to my forthcoming church wedding which was in those days, the only way to get legally married in Spain. At six o'clock on a cold February morning, avoiding the prying eyes of the early-rising-churchgoing-old-ladies, I was baptized in the same church where I was to be married two months later. I stood there, facing the altar, among the melting, dying candles from the previous day and under the eyes of the sad, bored and indifferent Saints displayed around the aisles. My Godfather was Alfonso, my best buddy from my army days; my Godmother my future mother-in-law. As a punishment for former and future sins, the priest splashed my head with a spurt of freezing water. The whole ceremony took less than ten minutes.

My mother's younger sister Marisa was born in 1922. She was not very bright but she was cheerful and as beautiful as Ava Gardner (though much shorter). She was single and worked as a typist at the Law Courts; she was also very independent, not the perfect housekeeper, nor a lover of children. Consequently, she flirted with many, married none then hung out indefinitely with Julian, who was her senior by many years, and whom she met when she was still very young. In the end, the relationship crumbled when he financially and sentimentally ruined her.

She laughed when she said, "When you get married you fuck it."

She lived in a cosy guest house called the *Pensión Roso*, located in Marqués de Cubas street, in one of the best districts of the capital, opposite the American Express Travel Services, the Palace Hotel and the Parliament. She was a working girl, way ahead of her time, an obvious contrast to the traditional, puritan Spain of the forties. She smoked her Chesterfield cigarettes in the street (unheard of for a woman), dressed impeccably with a hat, and used an exclusive perfume whose aroma impregnated the letters she wrote to us on thin, blue airmail paper, with a clear, fine hand, wound up with an elegant signature.

Her beauty and style didn't pass unnoticed when she strolled along the fancy Serrano and Goya streets. She was one of the privileged in wretched post war Spain.

In the late forties, my grandfather, a worker handling linotypes, had started his own business with Julian's financial help. It was a small but profitable family business: a metal foundry for the manufacture of the bars and blocks made of tin and lead alloy used in those days by magazines, newspapers and book publishers to carve the characters (metal letters) which were assembled first in lines and pages for printing. The workers used giant metal spoons to pour the boiling silvery liquid from the large cauldrons where both metals had been melted, into heavy iron moulds. When the blocks were ready, they were knocked out of the moulds with a hammer; stacked until they cooled, loaded into a van and delivered to the half dozen printing companies that formed the backbone of the clientele.

My aunt resigned from her job and joined her father. She answered the phone, helped with the paperwork and took care of their relations with the bankers whom she considered, before anyone else did, as a bunch of scoundrels and thieves.

In 1956 while we were in Egypt, my grandfather fell ill with prostate cancer. When he died in 1957, Aunt Marisa took over the business with the help of Julian, who had been recently fired from the Ministry of Commerce for his many misdeeds.

Julian, Marisa's lifelong sweetheart, was fifteen years her senior. He spent most of the Spanish Civil War on the loser's side (the Republican side) but defected before the end of the conflict and jumped unscathed into Franco's winning camp.

He was a compulsive gambler a liar and a no-good swindler. As the only investor and lover, he crawled into Marisa's business and finally wrecked it by keeping most of the foundry's income which he gambled away or bestowed upon his unemployed, useless rascal friends who were always sniffing around, ready for a kill.

In those days, gambling was forbidden in Spain and he often vanished for days, to gratify his vice, into the Casino of the French town of Biarritz.

In 1967 he used the power of attorney she unthinkingly gave him, to sell without her consent the foundry and the land it stood on to real estate developers who demolished the premises and built a five storey building. He kept the money and disappeared, forsaking a thirty-year relationship. He totally ruined her except for an apartment she luckily kept, and which now belongs to my family.

Julian finally re-appeared six years later; he had been living in Buenos Aires with his sisters. He had terminal prostate cancer, could hardly walk and was wheeled in a chair through Madrid airport. Like a rogue elephant, he had returned to the old country to die. One month later, we read his obituary in the newspaper; my aunt seemed unaffected. She was a practical woman and apparently she had forgotten.

After the Civil War, Julian had secured an important position as secretary to the secretary to the Minister of Industry, from which he was fired a few years later. He had married during the Republic. It was a civil marriage and therefore declared null and void after the war, as only Catholic ceremonies were legally recognised by the new fascist state. It saved them the cost of a divorce, as he and his wife split up just before the end of the conflict.

He hated blacks, apparently because his daughter had married a black American serviceman, or because he thought she had wedded the largest, blackest and meanest Air Force Sergeant stationed at the Torrejón de Ardoz air base on the outskirts of Madrid. But to prove he was no racist and didn't resent his son in law, he also hated Asians, Indians, half-breed of any kind and hairy hippies whom he thought of as a bunch of faggots. No-one was safe when that man was around. He also had a son somewhere, but I don't think he was on speaking terms with either of them.

His privileged post at the Ministry gave him access to rare and precious import licences which were the legal counterpart of the black market. He used some to import Swiss watches and sold the rest of the licences to his friends.

To appreciate this unusual situation, one has to understand that in post civil war Spain, people were deprived of most basic needs. Spanish industry had been destroyed and not yet rebuilt. Employment was scarce and the country sunk to nineteenth century standards. The poor starved and searched in garbage cans for potato peelings or any other waste they could lay their hands on. A friend recently told me that he saw his neighbours in the country, dig up and eat a decomposing mule that had been dead for days.

Well into the sixties, Spaniards emigrated en masse, looking for blue-collar jobs in Germany, France, Holland, Belgium and Switzerland. Those were the boom years in post World War Two Europe and eager hands were badly needed to rebuild shattered economies. Other Spaniards seeking a permanent exile sailed to Mexico, Argentina and Brazil. Those with Republican affiliations had fled the country after the war to avoid persecution, imprisonment and execution.

Imported goods were difficult to obtain, even for the rich, because the government lacked the necessary hard currency to pay for them; import licences were thus the only legal way to release the coveted dollars. Goods ranging from motorcycles to baby food were brought in from Europe and America, and sold to the well entrenched old wealth, as well as to the nouveaux riches who had thrived thanks to their black market activities during and after the Civil War.

Julian was a master of the art of embezzlement and had a *pico de oro* (golden mouthed). My aunt was bewildered and seduced by seniority, his experiences and his know-how oozing from his foul mouth; she swallowed his lies like mother's milk.

He was small, bald and unattractive, but intelligent and charismatic although because of the many dark sides of his character, he was unworthy as a person. He probably thought I was a spoiled little brat (which I was), when aged thirteen I pulled a chair from under him, when he was sitting down, and he landed on his arse on the floor. And he must have considered me a blockhead, when at twenty and looking seventeen, I came to Madrid with a face covered in pimples and a head filled with fantasies, still believing in rose gardens having learned nothing from my few experiences in Alexandria or those of my parents, in the midst of that once rich and cosmopolitan atmosphere, which in the end turned into an empty and distressed shell.

My father, who talked little but was a sharp observer of human nature, never liked Julian. My mother loathed him; she knew that sooner or later, he would wreck her sister, and he finally did. Nevertheless, my aunt, who had always been lucky, started a new life in the late sixties, and raised three little girl cousins who had lost their parents in an air crash; she didn't like children but ended up being a good surrogate mother to them. She was a heavy smoker and died at seventy-eight of lung cancer.

CHAPTER FIVE

My parents met at a party in Madrid in 1940, during the Second World War. I cannot, even by the wildest stretch of the imagination, picture my father swinging to the sound of the forties Big Bands or slinking his way around the floor to the rhythm of Spanish and South American sweet languid melodies, which were the flavour of the day; but then maybe he didn't dance and just stood there, watching.

He had a Bachelor of Arts degree, knew five languages and an amateur archaeologist. He was also a philosopher and like all philosophers, he was apparently calm, sometimes angry and often depressed, as he realised that the nature of man is despairing and undeserving of any study, and that the pursuit of wisdom and the understanding of values serves no purpose, as there isn't any.

The philosopher's quest is hopeless, because no philosophical equation or logical reasoning will ever arise, to explain the stupidity and the weakness of human kind, which breeds greed, envy, selfishness, cruelty, aggressiveness, constant fear of death and other cats, all dishonourable but necessary traits which have preserved man from destruction and extinction, and helped him thrive to become not only the number one predator, but also the sick cell consuming the body from which it has sprung.

The earth will always be there as long as the solar system exists; through eternity, it has survived many natural catastrophes, much worse than man can ever inflict. Whether man will survive is uncertain.

There are no "whys" to ponder on, or to be solved, and creation is nothing but an absurd, mysterious, transitional accident, with no beginning and no end. If one doesn't accept this fact, one will be at one's most vulnerable and easy prey for the "loving arms" of established religions as well as preachers and swindlers of all sorts who will provide the stupid and the weak, with illuminating answers to explain the unexplainable and provide temporary solace until one is dead and gone and nothing matters anymore. The strength of religions is that the dead don't file complaints. Nothing is proved, but nothing is disproved either.

The Big Bang theory is also hard to swallow; but for the scientists, it was necessary to explain the birth of the universe in time and space, and to provide a smart alternative to God. Man's brain can only function on three pillars of thought: time, space and rationality. The Big Bang thus came in very handy to explain at least, two of these three factors. As we all know the theory explains that before the big bang, there was no time or space and the matter forming our present universe, which is huge and boundless, was condensed into a singularity that occupied no time or space. This singularity must have been smaller than a pinpoint, a non-entity, a *nada*. The singularity exploded, creating space, time and all the matter in the universe. I am no scientist and my knowledge of physics is elementary, but I refuse to believe that all the matter (or the energy) forming the universe can be squeezed together and reduced to "almost" nothing. Even black holes which are formed by highly compressed matter and which by no means contain all the cosmos, occupy a specified space and can been identified.

This theory also needed to be explained. Fortunately for the scientists the Hubble space telescope was able to transmit to earth the "echo" of the Big Bang fifteen billion years ago, when it was still perceptible and reverberating throughout the universe, waiting for our good pleasure. (This echo business reminds me of the efforts of the investigators of the Warren Commission, after the Kennedy assassination, trying to convince the witnesses on the scene of the murder that the many shots they heard were just the "echoes" of the three acknowledged and official shots). The Big Bang theory is a "scientific religion" explaining the beginning of time and space.

Curious but irrational minds can rest assured after they're told that energy has the power to indefinitely multiply itself into matter and vice-versa, a sort a primeval sophisticated version of the bread and fishes miracle. If one believes in God, why not believe in the Big Bang and accept this singularity as God Himself Who exploded and filled a universe which wasn't there before. I think however that this is an insult to intelligence and common sense, as much as religions are an offence to God if God exists.

But it doesn't matter much, and no-one will be punished as His existence is quite improbable. The Church ratifies the Big Bang theory as it coincides with their belief that God created the Universe in one go and out of nothing. If we are to understand the ways of the universe we will, not through equations, but using our imagination, which travels faster than the speed of light. Speculations are fine, but they are just speculations, and no one will ever understand the immensity of a universe which has no beginning and no end in time and space.

True philosophers, past and present, are unheard because they never spoke, speak or will speak out their mind. They are born and they die, and they don't write or preach or teach or holler or explain or complain. They are the silent witnesses of world's follies. They just do their bit of thinking and when their time comes, they pass away quietly, plunging into the eternity of nothingness, with no fear or grudges or remorse. I am sure this is how my father lived and died.

Dad always knew of the precariousness and absurdity of existence and the falseness of the concepts and the values we take for granted. He referred to his own philosophy as *filosofía barata* (armchair philosophy) and I now know that's the only philosophy there is. The arts and intelligent entertainment are, for the mentally enriched, fountains of solace producing brief moments of happiness and making life sometimes worthwhile and bearable. I maintain that if you find five minutes of happiness a day, you can consider yourself a happy man.

The end of the story and the only consolation is that when death finally closes in, one's treasured earthly possessions become worthless and trivial, and one's "everlasting" feelings and attachments towards dear ones are no more. The weariness of the exhausted body and mind, longing for infinite state of nothingness, becomes the only reality. The "end of the world" occurs when your own life ends. If you live for one more hour or forty more years, that span is the countdown to the end of the world as far as you're concerned. It's also the final and total act of selfishness.

Since 1939, my father had been living and working in Tetuán, the capital of what was once Spanish Morocco, as a tutor in the household of the Caliph, (who could be compared to a Maharajah during the British Raj in India) and through whom Spaniards ruled their Protectorate.

In 1940 he and two Egyptian friends who had joined him from Cairo, one the portrait painter Hussein Bikar were spending a holiday in Paris when the Germans invaded France, and were only a few days away from Paris. The three Egyptian Caballeros swiftly jumped across the border into neutral Spain and hurried to Madrid with the idea of catching a train to the southern coastal town of Algeciras, (in Arabic *Al Ghazira* means the island, though it isn't one) and board a ferry across the Straits of Gibraltar to Morocco.

However, though his two friends finally managed to return to Egypt, my father lingered in Madrid. He was granted a scholarship and spent months with my mother-to-be, in the prestigious Library of the El Escorial Monastery, a palace located fifty kilometres northwest of Madrid and a former residence of the Kings of Spain. While the war was raging, he studied the ancient Arab and Jewish books and manuscripts in the hush of the Library. He also talked with the Prior and the local pundits, sharing ideas and comparing cultures, in those serene, restful surroundings, which were a huge contrast to what was occurring in war devastated Europe. He took a leave of absence from his Morocco post and stayed in Spain for a couple of years to woo my mother. In 1942 he married her at the Egyptian Consulate in Tangiers and they returned to Tetuán, to a new home and a new life.

CHAPTER SIX

In civilised nations racism is concealed behind a varnish of hypocrisy and good manners that crack when challenging circumstances arise. Racism subsists since man, at the dawn of his existence, had to exterminate lesser human breeds sharing his living space and standing in his way to survival and expansion. This practice has remained constant through the ages and is joyfully carried out today in many countries.

In the forties, continental Spain was still quite unconcerned with religious or racial issues as the country was isolated and backward with no foreign immigrants to push the button of hate and intolerance. Yet, in the Capital of Spanish Morocco, windy Tetuán by the sea, racism was rampant. Mother went nuts and cursed all Spaniards each time the postman (to denigrate my father's name and religion) called out loud for everyone in the building to hear, "Mail for the Muslim Mohamed", while climbing the stairs to our apartment or ringing our door bell.

In those days Mom disliked "the Spain" she had just left, a post-war shattered country. She loathed the late Republic and the three-year civil war she had endured. She hated the communists—especially the fanatical Dolores Ibarruri who yearned to turn Spain into a Soviet Satellite. Known as the Pasionaria this female leader urged women to practise free love and have "fatherless children". She also said that the old should be eliminated because they ate young people's bread.

My mother remembered well the Red hoodlums ripping apart and burning Spanish banners swinging Russian flags with hammer and sickle and chanting Russian slogans. She despised the socialists and the anarchists and the International Brigades that bunch of soldiers of fortune from Europe and America who came to Spain to fight for "democracy" but mostly to screw the red-hot-free-women of the Republic who had dropped their knickers after the collapse of the Monarchy and the debacle of the Church, and were fucking their brains out right and left, enjoying their new-found freedom as if there were no tomorrow, which there wasn't, though they didn't know it yet.

She also abominated all the far-left parties selfishly fighting each other for power. But above all, she hated the "scum of the earth", those masses of poor, illiterate, envious, cruel and vengeful crowds that had jumped out of the gutters like big threatening and hungry rats, shielded behind the turbulence and chaos, when war started and law and order were no more

She despised her father and her uncles and her cousins for accusing her of marrying a *moro* (moor is the name still used in Spain to call all Arabs, as if they were still obsessed by the Arab Berbers, who conquered and occupied the country for eight centuries and left a deep moral and physical imprint that many Spaniards prefer to ignore).

Her family accused her not only of marrying a moor but for leaving home to wed (if she actually ever did) in some God-forgotten shabby North African Town. They considered her behaviour disgraceful and her insolence inadmissible. The good conservative church-going family was shocked. It was something unheard of in the Saintly and

Chaste Spain of 1942 recently purged by Franco's crusade (the Civil War) from evil and atheism. The Generalissimo's deeds were linked to the exploits of the Catholic Monarchs, who freed the country from the Jews and the Arabs achieving the imposed union of all the Spanish provinces. What an adventure!!!

They were convinced that my mother's behaviour was caused by an isolated virus which had triggered a nasty rebellion against the institutions and Mother Church which were one and the same. Their verdict was like an autodafé: "To the stake with her" they unanimously agreed.

The trouble with them was unhealthy and forbidding envy, Spain's worst defect, an incurable dark sickness which has tainting the country for centuries. The poor naturally envy the wealthy, but the prosperous often envy the less fortunate, if they believe that the latter have any kind of edge on them.

The family had met my father, who was intelligent and gracious, sensitive and cultured while they were only "white trash with money" or "pieces of meat with eyes" which is my favourite expression to classify that kind of people. They envied Mom because she was leaving a gloomy, miserable and uncertain future in Spain, to live in a country they mistakenly thought of as the "Arabian nights", a land of milk and honey.

My mother and her sister Marisa were contemplated by the rest of the family as "Cinderellas" because they were penniless working girls, poor offspring of a dead mother and a careless father who had forsaken them to live with his mistress. They thought, therefore, that my mother was undeserving of any good luck, not even a small break. They believed that luck and breaks were the privilege of the rich. The destitute deserved nothing.

She partly made her peace with her kin, when in 1948 we came to Madrid for a few months just before we departed for Egypt as they realised that we were leaving for a long, long time, probably for ever. However Mom never forgave or forgot the humiliations she endured; she surely knew how to hate when they pushed her hard. But what's the use of wronging when the wrongdoers and wronged are all dead.

However, she often talked with certain longing of her three cousins, children of her rich uncle José her aunt's husband, when she read about them in her sister's letters. Aurora the brunette—also called fatty—was engaged to an army sergeant who later rose from the ranks to become a Captain. While on duty, he was fond of keeping a pair of her dirty knickers in his uniform pocket to enjoy the smell as if they were a perfumed hanky (I was informed of that indiscretion in Madrid); Anita, blonde, beautiful and futile married a penniless lawyer who, with great skill, built a brilliant career with the money his wife received from his father-in-law; Pepito, the youngest and only son inherited from his father at twenty-seven and never did an honest day's work in his life; when the old man died they all shared an inheritance equivalent to one hundred and eighty thousand euro, a colossal amount by 1959 Spanish standards.

Egypt's economy was controlled by the Egyptian ruling classes (descendants of the Ottomans) and by "Egyptian foreigners" (called *khawagat*) who had been in Egypt for generations. That melting pot which included Italians, Greeks, Armenians, Jews, Levantines and other minorities, pulled the strings and held the bridles of the country through their culture, wealth and know-how. Most of these *khawagat* arrived in Egypt either fleeing from the disturbance, insecurities and poverty of nineteenth and early twentieth century Europe or to escape Christian persecution in the *Sham* (Syria and Lebanon) as well as ethnic cleansing of Armenians in the former Ottoman Empire. All these people had embraced the habits and the tastes of their adoptive country. They ate Egyptian food and behaved in many ways as natives, but they treated the lower indigenous Arabs with contempt. Most of them spoke perfect Arabic while others had accents. From one generation to the other they thought that Egypt was for keeps and cried their eyes out (especially the Jews) when their time was over and they were forced out of country into permanent exile.

Amongst the *khawagat* religion was unimportant, not an issue in everyday relations. One never looked into the religious beliefs of a friend or schoolmate. At the Lycée we all received a laic education according to the principles of the *Mission Laïque Française,* on which our school was founded. Many of our companions were Jews with surnames like Cohen, Franco and Israel. One of them, although named Sammy, was never regarded as Jewish—not even by our Jew classmates—because his surname was Ibrahim which is typically Arab and Muslim but translates in Hebrew to Abraham. It simply didn't matter what one's religion was.

Egyptian Jews loved Egypt very deeply, possibly in the same way Sephardic Jews cherished medieval Spain before their expulsion. The Egyptian revolution of 1952, which brought to power a military dictatorship, made them pay very dearly for living in a country that wasn't theirs and that could not come to terms with the new State of Israel. Could things have turned out differently for the Jews and for the rest of the Khawagat had Israel not been founded? I don't think so. Sooner or later, Egypt had to return to its original roots.

Before the revolution, the Egyptian ruling class and European minorities held property rights over agriculture (cotton, tobacco, cereal, rice, sugar, etc.) and the industries that processed such products. They also controlled commerce, import-export, real estate, department stores, pharmaceuticals and all major activities which kept the country running. But these people were living a dream which they took for granted. It wasn't reality just a delusion, a make believe like a movie set which is dismantled or abandoned when the shooting of the film is completed. They had created a dreamland for themselves, a cosmopolitan multi-lingual, multi-religious society in the middle of a poor, simple and light-hearted native population whom they treated as inferiors. These had accepted the mild bondage, because of the employment and the menial jobs the khawagat provided. Nevertheless, the people of Egypt longed for self-respect, the chance to recover their full identity and to be able to live, to behave and to rule their country as they thought best.

On my trip to Alexandria, in November 2010, I noticed that all traces of our foreign past had been totally erased with the exception of a few old-time spots like the Greek Clubs hosts to an ever-shrinking community of Greeks, now down to eight-hundred from a former prosperous community of more than one hundred thousand. These Clubs also cater for the eating and drinking habits of wealthy and educated Egyptians who seek the peace of an alien oasis in the midst of the surrounding noisy and hectic masses. Watching the dense indigenous populace roaming the streets: fully or partially covered women, bearded fundamentalists (Alexandria is the cradle of fundamentalism), unfriendly faces, hearing the background noise of loudspeakers tied to lampposts calling for daily prayers, seeing the shattered façades, and becoming aware of a creeping smell of garbage and not a European in sight, it was impossible to conceive that fifty years ago the city was a sophisticated metropolis where French, Greek and Italian were the semi-official languages. That fictitious society built by one time immigrants was no more; their dream lasted as long as it lasted, i.e. until history revolved and dropped them for good.

Alexandria has now returned to its original and true roots which are those of a Mediterranean North African Muslim city seasoned by a minority of Copts (the Christian Egyptians who were living in Egypt long before it became a Muslim country), who represent approximately ten percent of Egypt's population. Wandering again through those familiar streets after forty-six years of absence, I felt as if my life there had been an illusion, as if everything I had experienced for many years had never occurred.

The elegant downtown movie houses and their neighbourhood counterparts are in a state of decrepitude and exhibit only Egyptian pictures. Half a century ago, in those same cinemas, I built my dreams and stimulated my fantasies through hundreds of American movies which kept my spirit high almost as much as my "alma mater", the Lycée Français, expanded my horizons with a first-class education.

The Egyptian middle and lower classes are permanently struggling with all their wits (and they have many) to survive within an economy and an environment they cannot understand or change, and which is getting the best of them. The efforts of the majority are wasted in the hopelessness of corruption, inefficiency and disorder, breeding anger, frustration and discontent amongst the population. A humorous, pastry-shopkeeper confessed:

"The pressure I'm bearing on my shoulders is so strong that I'm getting shorter every day".

The *fellaheen* (peasants) backbone of the country, have been living on the banks of the River Nile for thousands of years and work their lump of land which at times is not sufficient to feed their families. Nevertheless, they take many wives, breed countless children, blame the Government for their misfortunes and thank Allah for what they have.

In his early twenties, my father flirted with a fashionable new ideology called communism which was sweeping through Europe after the end of the First World War. It was fashionable for young intellectuals to study and experiment with this new concept as it was in the sixties for the youth of the free world to use marijuana, LSD and hashish. Dad was a naïve humanist and probably believed as many others did that the promised "worker's paradise" would help to ease the injustices and miseries suffered by many societies in the world and by Egyptian society in particular. As a philosopher, he considered the matter solely from a theoretical point of view. He never went deep or participated in its diffusion. His curiosity and interest were superficial. He scratched and studied the bases of communism, and pondered on how these fresh, red ideas from Eastern Europe seemed a good pointer to ending all wars and building a better humanity which he thought was emerging from the Great War, considered then the bloodiest of all wars. He wasn't yet "crushed by the ways of the world" and probably still cared for the welfare and future of man, which is a very noble but also a very candid, exhausting and useless cause, considering how low and undeserving human nature is.

Since the age of consciousness one is thrown into a multicoloured and pitiless arena, a dysfunctional zoo filled with predators and prey: trained monkeys in business suits, husky, hairy bears in blue overalls, dirty rats, fickle weasels, crawling worms, gluttonous pigs, insolent bitches, menacing buzzards, treacherous sharks, submissive sheep, astute little foxes, and, happily for us all, a few brave, noble and intelligent lions.

Mark Twain who they say hated mankind but loved people (I wish I could say the same) wrote in his then unpublished memoirs: "Mankind was not made for any useful purpose, for the reason that he hasn't served any". How right he was when he wrote that piece, more than one hundred years ago, when the miseries that man foisted on his surrounding were not yet as evident as they are today. In the long run, the only possibility for the survival of the world as an assembly of species is for our own species to disappear. But man is the top predator and a survivor. He won't give up easily unless he is violently shaken and pushed overboard by extreme circumstances such as wild actions of nature or clusters of asteroids from outer space. Will man shut the world before the world shuts him? I'm glad I won't be here to find out.

Earth has no memory and no feelings and it's old enough and big enough and pitiless enough to swallow mankind without leaving a single trace of his follies and misfortunes. But all things considered, what is the use of any of the species from the largest to the smallest? Their use or their reason to exist is that they live life for life, one day at the time not thinking of the past or dreaming of the future and totally unconscious of death. That's good enough for me. However the negative facet of man—which makes him undesirable, compared to the rest of creation—is that he destroys whatever stands on his way to fulfil his relentless greed and his senseless faculty of reproduction.

By taking an interest in communism, my father maybe "dreamed" to freeing his country from the oppression and the inequalities endured for centuries, first at the hands of the Ottoman ruling class and, since the end of the nineteenth century, under the rule of the British. The Cairo riots of 1919, when the crowds cried out their discontent, their hatred of imperialism and their desire for freedom and home rule had something to do with it, as he was seventeen when these events happened.

He had studied Marx but hardly remembered what he read and in random conversations he spoke about the "the ABC of communism". But he soon gave up this unrewarding trail, and built around himself a wall of indifference as a sterling protection against the deplorable mediocrity of others and as a safeguard from unhappiness.

Before taking the course which led him to a teaching career he had tried other ventures and indulged in other vocations, pharmacology being one of them. He also wrote travel accounts and essays which he never published. Maybe he wasn't confident of his talent as a writer or because he preferred to write for his pleasure only as an escape from his unrewarding and somehow degrading daily job which didn't match his abilities. He didn't give much for recognition or money and was probably afraid to speak his mind in a society governed by state police and censorship.

My mother once told me that he had been swindled by a "friend" who borrowed one of his manuscripts, never returned it and later published it as his own. He wrote in the evenings, when he returned from work but I never asked him what he was writing about; I lacked the basic curiosity and he often looked distant and unconcerned.

Although his pen kept flowing, his fountain of love had dried out a long time before—or maybe it was never there.

He was a difficult man to understand and now that he's dead and I've almost reached the age he was when he passed away, it's not easy either.

Egypt was for men with initiative, strength and courage the country of opportunities. The entrepreneurs, industrialists, businessmen and professionals were mostly Jews, Armenians, Greeks and Italians who thrived for more than a hundred years.

At the end of the Second World War, my father could have emigrated to the United States or Canada which were much more suitable countries for a man of substance and where his intellectual capacities would have been recognised and appreciated. He possessed the necessary qualifications to try for a better life, but he lacked the taste for adventure and the energy and ambition required for such an endeavour.

Perhaps I am wrong to judge him by my own standards, without considering his feelings and his material needs (which were few). He was a pessimist as befits an intelligent man and didn't hope for much, except to "pass quietly through life", as most people do, except that he knew and accepted that basic and only truth better than anyone else.

Instead of looking for a new life elsewhere when his time in Tetuán was up in 1948, he returned to an unfulfilled Egyptian life. I was no fool and always detected in his eyes the shades if bitterness and discontent which he bore like an incurable and consuming malady. He disliked the heat and the sun and the *khamseen* (a hot spring wind, lasting up to fifty days, hence the name, meaning fifty in Arabic), and the dust and the noise and the flies and the fat, flying brown cockroaches, which landed in our bedrooms on those torrid Summer nights when the windows were open. He also hated crowds, which are worse than flies, because they are dirtier and noisier and nastier and can't be wiped out or crushed with the palm of the hand. *Emshe emshe* (go away, go away), was the favourite expression of the *khawagat*, to dismiss the obtrusive natives when they came too close or got out of line.

Dad was a loner and in his late thirties, looked like a displaced Arthur Miller lost in a sea of shit, which was the country where he was born, lived and worked but to which he never belonged. Sometimes they called him *effendi* (sir) but most of the time he was a *khawaga*. He must have felt like an outcast when, as soon as we arrived to Egypt, in the late forties and fifties he was dispatched as a teacher and later headmaster to muddy and backward villages along the Nile, the most civilised of all being the town of Luxor, in Upper Egypt where we spent a couple of years. Many lives are lost and end up drowning in mediocrity and the regrets of unfulfilled dreams.

The fear of failure and the efforts and the sacrifices required to achieve one's ambitions curtail the possibility of success and consequently the enjoyment of a richer and more satisfying life. If the mind fuelled by imagination seems ready for action, the inertia and the negativism of the body holds back any undertaking. Frustration, anguish, rage, bitterness and finally depression follow at the end of the line because of the incapacity to attain one's ambitions according to one's vocation or desires. Nothing remains then, except to live as if one didn't exist, but even then, one will always feel that things will not turn out better but worse. Finally, when age takes it toll and the end of the road is perceivable, and when dreams are long dead and buried, only total indifference can save you from despair.

During the hot Egyptian spring, early summer and autumn, while working in those God forgotten villages, my father sweated so profusely that he frequently suffered from dehydration, was afflicted with cramps in his hands and feet and lost large amounts of salt which he replaced by eating salty dishes.

I know almost nothing of his early years. He was almost forty when he met my mother and fifty when I started at seven or eight to become observant of things and people. He was introverted, spoke little and was considered by those who knew him as a *ragel tayeb* (good man).

In the late forties, corporal punishment in schools was a practice which was not only permitted, but advised and encouraged by parents and teachers alike. My father, as headmaster, would summon the wrongdoers to his office and cane them several times on the buttocks with a ruler or a long, thin wooden stick. Whenever I called on him I saw fear and anguish in the eyes of the boys standing there at attention, moments before the fateful caning ceremony began. His colleagues apparently respected him. He was so "alien" to them that, as far as they were concerned, he might have landed from another galaxy.

CHAPTER SEVEN

I was born at home (which was the proper thing to do) in Tetuán, on Friday 16th June 1944 at 05.00 hours. It was considered by the locals as good timing and a lucky omen, as this time of day coincides with the weekly firing of the garrison cannon calling the faithful to the first prayer on the Muslim day of rest.

I don't know how but my father managed to register me as if I were born in Madrid. This ruse turned out to be useful, when at twenty-one, I applied for Spanish nationality. After hours of unfruitful labour, forceps were reluctantly used for delivery. I weighed over four kilos and my mother—a petite woman of five feet—complained later that by lifting and carrying me I wrecked her back for life. She later developed a hunchback which kept her bent her forward and, when she got very old (she lived to be ninety) affected her standing and walking.

My father, who witnessed the painful ordeal of my birth, vehemently refused to go through this same experience again and wisely decided that I would be an only child. It was also an excuse as good as any other, as he did not like or tolerated kids (my aunt Marisa teasingly called him King Herod).

I came to sympathise with his choice and reckoned that he had made the right decision as soon as I reached maturity and was conscious of the absurdity and uselessness of existence. One of nature's traps is to bestow on the young a strong libido and a silly state of mind in order to achieve the one and only thing nature is interested in: the reproduction and survival of the species.

But mother didn't concur with my father's wishes and wanted at least one more child. She loved children and was oblivious of the pitfalls. She didn't understand the economic implications children brought and the burden an additional child would add to the meagre budget of the household. Women are made to think that way (the call of nature) and intelligent men are there to restrain them. Maybe she was not aware of the advantages of only sons, who are more imaginative more intelligent and more independent. But she was headstrong and persisted in her quest. She proved totally senseless and insensitive when, years later, she tried to become pregnant by piercing with a needle, tiny holes in the condoms my father used and which he kept in a bedroom drawer.

Later, when I married and my mother was living with us in Madrid, she confided to my wife about her little indiscretion and I was stunned when my wife told me. She had been selfish and inconsiderate. She wasn't a bread-winner and acted with total disregard for his (my father's) feelings without a thought for our financial situation, which was never buoyant. If she had succeeded in her intent my father would have looked stupid, like a sucker unable to use his condoms properly. She would have probably blamed the condom manufacturers for carelessness. She intended to face him with a *fait accompli*, a possibility he refused to consider or to accept as he wanted to protect his privacy, his peace of mind and his resources. Fortunately for us, Egyptian prophylactics were indestructible; they were made of latex, as thick and resistant as orthopaedic stockings and nothing could break through those sons of bitches. Obviously sensitivity and pleasure were not the main issue.

Such significant decisions must be discussed and approved by both partners and never become a one-side choice. She disregarded him and only thought of herself, attempting to mislead a good, honest man, something which is shameful, inadmissible behaviour. If I had know as a child what I was told later, my feelings for her would have surely been diminished, with loss of love and respect, which could have signified quite an ordeal for my mental well-being and self-confidence during my decisive childhood years.

I was named Chérif, a Muslim and Christian name meaning noble. Family and friends called me "Cherry" which back then didn't sound sissy. In 1965, when I applied for Spanish citizenship, I changed it to Ricardo.

I don't remember much of my childhood in Tetuán, except that I was the cause and focus of stormy rows between my parents. My father was once determined to spank me when I flung to the living-room floor three full shelves containing his treasured books. I tried his patience again when with the help of my beach shovel I almost succeeded in uprooting the bedroom door from its hinges; at two or three years old it was quite a *tour de force.* It was a heavy, solid pine-wood door that could have killed me had it fallen on me. My mother strongly opposed this medieval punishment and threatened to show him hell or even worse if he insisted on beating an "innocent" child.

The images and sounds of those quarrels echoed intensely in my small head. The resonance of their voices and incomprehension of the reality were overwhelming as I sat on the floor watching above me their fight of titans. They finally worked out a peace plan and I became untouchable for the remainder of my restless childhood.

From our balcony facing the street and situated on the second floor of the building, we once watched a motorcycle Grand Prix held on the town streets and passing in front of our house. The competition was halfway through when one of the racers lost control of his machine while taking a sharp bend and smashed his head on the kerb, only a few metres from where we were watching. When they finally managed to remove his helmet his crushed head split open like a ripe melon adroitly cut by expert hands and his brains spilled, like salad dressing, all over the pavement.

Windy Tetuán by the sea was more a colonial borough than a real city. Half Spanish and half Arab, the two factions despised each other but life went on. My mother suffered from frequent migraines which she blamed on the constant wind. She was also vulnerable to stomach trouble that came and went according to her mood. She had a nervous condition brought on I think, by a state of discontent. She was a housewife and a mother but probably yearned for something more. I think she liked the town and the social status conferred on her as a Spaniard in a Spanish colony and the wife of a tutor in the Caliphs' household.

My aunt visited regularly from Madrid, which was a relief for her as she tired of listening to my father, his friends and colleagues talk in Arabic, a language she couldn't understand, but which she learned later in Egypt. She loved children and when we settled in Alexandria she nursed and took care of a new-born girl the daughter of her friend Afaf, who at seventeen, married a man who tripled her age. Afaf was also the kid sister of Lula Baraka and her husband, our Victoria district neighbours when we settled in Alexandria and my father's best friends. She accused Egyptian mothers of being irresponsible towards their children lacking the know-how in the ways of bringing them up.

After the Spanish Civil war and as a contribution to the peace efforts the *Servicio Social* (community work for women) became compulsory in Spain. From the age of eighteen every female had to serve the country for up to one year. They could choose amongst different activities such as office work, cooking and sewing for the poor, caring for the old and sick, or nursing children. My mother went for the latter whereas my aunt favoured paperwork in a Ministry. This service to the state was unavoidable and had to be completed if a girl wished to apply for a passport, look for a job or get married.

My mother also wrote fairy tales about mermaids with long tails. She loved the sea and the warm sandy beaches, inspiration for her stories. Maybe she wished she was a mermaid to move freely under the seas and eat lots of fish, her favourite food.

In 1948, my father was recalled home by his Ministry of Education. He had been away from Egypt for eight years and had missed the Second World War there, the razzmatazz of the British Army in Cairo and the nerve racking, uncertain months when the entry of Rommel's army into Alexandria and Cairo was imminent. A German victory was enthusiastically expected by the Egyptians, who wanted to get rid of British rule. It was feared by the European community and dreaded by the thousands of Jews who lived in Egypt and were getting ready to flee to South Africa. At the start of the war, and as soon as Mussolini joined the Germans, the Italian Community in Egypt was safely locked away by the British in concentration camps, to cool down their love and loyalty to the *Duce*. The Egyptian masses awaited the Germans whom they thought would deliver them from the British yoke. Late President Sadat was a notorious "resistant" specialised in explosives. He directed his underground operations against the British from a boat anchored on the river Nile.

Now in 1948, my father was uncertain of the Egyptian situation in those post-war years. He found soon enough that nothing had changed. The British were still in place, ruling the country. The wretched King Farouk was getting fatter and up to his usual misdeeds not yet knowing that his years were numbered.

My father left for Egypt months ahead of us and rented an apartment on the ground floor of a building in the district of Heliopolis (new district) in Cairo. He supposedly left earlier to take care of his ailing mother whom I never met. Maybe she passed away before our arrival.

Before our departure for Egypt, scheduled for May, we visited my aunt in Madrid. She was living as she always did in a guest house, but had rented an apartment for this special occasion. The flat was located on *Paseo Pintor Rosales* one of the finest districts in Madrid, overlooking the Rosales Park or the Western Park as it's often called. It wasn't far from the *Gran Via Avenue*, Madrid's main street, packed with cinemas, night clubs, cafeterias and shops and renamed in those days the *Avenida José Antonio* after the founder of the *Falange* fascist party, who was imprisoned and shot by the Republicans in Alicante during the Civil War. José Antonio Primo de Rivera was forsaken by Franco (a keen expert in eliminating would-be competitors) who refused to save him in an exchange of prisoners, as he considered him a dangerous rival in the future fascist Spain.

During the four months we spent in Madrid, my grandfather Bienvenido Tapia took me for strolls in the nearby park. I was the only grandchild he would ever have. When we met again in July 1957 he was terminally ill with prostate cancer. He looked emaciated and a shadow of his former self. He died in September at seventy-one in the same apartment which has been my home for the last forty-seven years.

My mother and I left for Egypt on 15th May, 1948 in a TWA four-engine Super Constellation New-York to Cairo flight with calls at Lisbon, Madrid, Rome and Athens. During the Rome and Athens one-hour stops, we stretched our legs on the tarmac while the plane was re-fuelled and serviced and new passengers heading for Cairo boarded. We walked around the aircraft, under the silver wings and the huge engines, which smelled of high-octane fuel. Those were the good old days free of safety measures. The brand new bicycle that my aunt bought for me was in the hold with the rest of the luggage or at least I so hoped, because I kept pointing at the belly of the carrier asking my mother if she was sure my bicycle was there.

After an eleven-hour journey we landed at Cairo airport. Our timing was lousy. The State of Israel had declared its independence that same day and the first major crisis between the Arabs and the Jews had just started. The scent of an imminent armed conflict was in the air. King Farouk and his cronies were dealing in faulty Italian weapons, such as hand grenades which blew-up in the faces of the soldiers, and back-firing, crooked rifles and guns. Not bad for a sideshow. It is believed that the king's treachery and his total disregard for his people or his country helped trigger the July 1952 revolution which brought the end to a Monarchy that had lasted since the times of the *Khedive* Mohamed Ali one hundred and fifty years before.

King Farouk went reluctantly to war with Israel. He knew, respected and appreciated the Jewish people as his father Kind Fuad also had, but was forced into this conflict by the young Arab League which had recently been created with Egypt as its leader. Egypt was indeed the strongest of the Arab countries and the only one able to challenge Israel with an organised, well-equipped army and British trained Officers.

The Egyptians had no grudge against Israel and no cause for a confrontation. Whether won or lost, this war was of no importance or consequence to them as they were not struggling for their survival as Israel was. The undeniable edge Israel will always have on its Arab neighbours is that Israelis fight for the existence of their country, while Arabs do it to satisfy the fancies and ambitions of one President or another, or for obscure political international manoeuvres they don't understand or care about. The armies of Egypt and the other Arab States participating in this war suffered a defeat and the State of Israel was established for good at a time in its history when it was most vulnerable and could have been wiped out, had the will and the courage and honesty of the Arab leaders been there to support their purpose. But these virtues were missing then, as they are now.

Egyptian Jews were mostly of Sephardic origin. They had come to Egypt from all over the Ottoman Empire where they had previously settled after their expulsion from Spain. Many were wealthy, while others just made a living; the businessmen, professionals and traders thrived while helping Egypt's economy.

Many *khawagat* were Egyptian Nationals while others, using influence and bribes, acquired European passports through the various Consulates in Alexandria. Some Jews never requested Egyptian or any other nationality and were thus stateless. Their only identification was a residence permit issued by the Egyptian authorities, which allowed them to reside and work in Egypt. What at first seemed to be an advantageous condition turned out to be a handicap, when between 1956 and 1967 they were definitively expelled and had no country to run to; as *apatrides* (stateless), the only country that would take them unconditionally was Israel, which some adopted as their new home, arriving there after a European or Cyprus detour as it was impossible and unimaginable at the time to travel there directly from Egypt. Those who wished to settle in Europe or America were assisted by the Jewish Communities. Franco's Spain, through the Spanish Consulate in Alexandria, granted to stateless Jews who so-wished, provisional Spanish passports to help with the immigration formalities in their host countries. Those passports had a validity of only two years, but provided the bearers with legal status in their new homelands until they legalized their situation and acquired resident's card or a new citizenship.

Franco, in times of internal political crisis especially in the forties and fifties, abused the Jews whom he accused—together with the Masons—of being mischievous and plotting against Spanish interests. His well-known condemnation, "the Jewish-Masonic conspiracy", was generally laughed at as being a scapegoat for the misfortunes of any nature afflicting the unstable country. But in spite of that, I always suspected him of being a bit Jewish of Sephardic descent. His features, his wits and his name spoke for it. Moreover, he extended his protection to the Spanish and Spain's-Moroccan Jews, when, during World War Two, his friend Hitler demanded (and he denied) their extradition to Germany for extermination. Or did he refuse because he thought of the consequences of such an act for him and his regime after the allies' victory? No one knows.

Franco didn't care for religion but he became during the Civil War (which he called "crusade") the undeniable champion of Catholicism, defeating and obliterating the dreadful Reds considered by the Church and the establishment alike as devils in disguise beget by the infamous womb of Mother Russia. Many people still don't realise what could have become of Spain if the Republic had won the Civil War or if the strife had never taken place.

The Second World War started in 1939 a few months after the end of the Spanish War. Logically, Spain would have sided with the allies especially after the Soviet Union was attacked by Germany and entered the conflict. After the war and the victory of the allies (Russia included) Spain would have become a Southern-European Soviet satellite in the heart of a free Europe, surrounded by democracies who, marshalled by the United States were soon involved in a cold war that would last for more than forty years. The country would have found itself more hopelessly isolated than it ever was with the Franco Regime, as any attempt by the democracies to overrun communist Spain would have meant direct confrontation with the Soviets, probably leading to a new world war. Spain would have been ostracized until the late eighties or early nineties when the countries belonging to the Soviet block recovered their independence.

The temperature in Cairo in that month of May was over forty degrees Celsius. While the day was dying, the aircraft dropped us after the last leg from Athens, on Cairo International Airport tarmac a few steps from the terminal building where my father and his nephew Fuad, dressed in his military uniform, were waiting. Fuad, then in his twenties, was an army lieutenant and was leaving the following day for the front where he was wounded a short time later. General Naguib, the first President of the future Republic of Egypt from 1952 to 1954, was also injured and became a war hero. Too many heroes and martyrs (the dead were considered martyrs) for a war which ended with the catastrophic defeat of the Egyptian army.

The presence of Fuad's uniform took us quickly and smoothly through Passport Control and Customs supervised by army officers as they still are today. The *zabet* (army officers) are sacred cows in Egypt. They are feared and respected, as they can pull their weight in all walks of life, police and secret services included. In wartime Egypt of 1948, their ego was as large as it got as they were the safeguard of the country. Four years later, after the success of the revolution their influence grew even stronger as Egypt became a military dictatorship.

Because of his lavish, carefree and selfish life-style, King Farouk was the perfect scapegoat; he was blamed for losing the war and for other misdeeds that had befallen the country and was finally toppled in 1952.

After the revolution, the colour of the Egyptian flag was changed from a vivid green to striped black, red and white: The colour Black stood for the dark days of the monarchy; white for the bloodless revolution; and red in tribute to the blood of the martyrs of past present and future, whoever they may be.

CHAPTER EIGHT

In Cairo, we settled into a ground floor apartment of a white building in the smart, exclusive district of Heliopolis that bordered the desert and was not far from the Lycée Français I started to attend a few months later.

During those war days blackouts were frequent not because of enemy bombings but to spare the population the sight of the dead and the wounded brought in from the front by special trains to Cairo Central Station. Egypt was taking a severe beating from a small new country whose pilots, flying obsolete airplanes dropped on Egyptian tanks home-made bombs that looked like Molotov cocktails. The repetitive hymn on the radio announcing the news was the triumphal march from the opera *Aida* composed for the inauguration of the Suez Canal—though Verdi couldn't finish it on time for this occasion and its first performance in public was two years later. Through listening to it at regular intervals, I came to believe that it was Egypt's National Anthem (I was recently told that it was indeed the National Anthem during King Farouk's reign).

I tirelessly rode my new bicycle I had brought all the way from Madrid and it was not long before I removed the two little wheels fixed on the back axle to help beginners to keep their balance. My next door neighbour Barbara was an English girl my age; she was blonde and twice my weight. She sometimes rode the bicycle but often preferred to sit her fat arse comfortably on the handlebars while I took her for quick trips around the block, proving my prowess and resistance by never giving up, even when I was breathless.

Our building bordered the desert and I watched a Bedouin on his camel coming out of nowhere (like Omar Sharif in his first scene of *Lawrence of Arabia*) for his weekly shopping. He hitched his camel to a lamp-post went into a grocery store and came out carrying two bulky saddlebags filled with goods. He mounted his camel, slowly rode away and disappeared over the horizon. I was puzzled as I couldn't picture anything more than what I could see. I wondered how he could live in the middle of nothingness. Where did man and camel come from, where did they go to after they were swallowed up by the desert sands?

I wasn't able to visualise that beyond that bleak horizon, there were green oases, water wells and Bedouin men, women and children tending sheep, sleeping in tents, drinking tea and smoking Camel cigarettes (sorry, I couldn't let this one pass). My view of the world was limited to what I saw, not to what I knew which was little. My imagination couldn't reach beyond that line, hardly visible on a misty day from where the man of the desert and his beast regularly appeared and over which they vanished later. It was a line that summarised my limited knowledge of life. My memories of happenings during my early months in Cairo are glued together at random like celluloid movie scenes cut and assembled by a careless editor. The situations I considered important got engraved in my memory and have remained there ever since.

While my parents were taking their daily afternoon siesta, the ice-cream man from *Groppi*, (the most renowned pastry-shop and tea-room in Cairo) used to come by riding his three-wheeler delivery bicycle with an ice-box attached. I would hang onto the window bars, ready and waiting, clutching some coins in my hand. As soon as I heard the familiar voice crying: "Ice . . . cream . . . . *Groppi* . . . ," I rushed outside and bought a chocolate or strawberry terrine. Those were very hot summer afternoons, and when he opened the cover of the ice-box a cold, multi-perfumed wave, a mixture of many flavours, slipped out and embraced me like the breeze of an air-conditioner. I thought of those magic moments as a sort of compensation for being watchful and silent while I waited for the man to come. The flavour and smell of the ice-cream that I so quickly ate lasted however, for a long time. How uncomplicated is a child's mind when his main concern revolves around such trivial issues.

One day, on my way back from an errand for my mother, I slipped and fell on the wet kitchen floor while holding in my left hand a green bottle of *spathis,* a soft sparkling beverage she drank to ease the stomach pains occasioned by a nervous condition. The bottle exploded and a piece of glass cut deeply into my hand, leaving my pinkie hanging in the wind. She called father, wrapped my bleeding hand in handkerchiefs and rushed me off in a taxi to the nearest hospital, where a young intern gave me nine stitches. The doctor praised my calm and courage. He had done the job without anaesthesia and I didn't raise hell by weeping or yelling; I just bit the bullet, endured the pain and didn't utter a word.

Another time while trying to climb Mount Everest in the shape of a seven-foot tall locker, I stumbled down and hurt my right arm. It rapidly swelled and doubled in size so my mother rubbed it with alcohol and wrapped it up in a bandage. No bones were broken and I was fit in a week. She took a chance there, as my arm could have been fractured but that's the way she was. She disliked and distrusted hospitals and doctors and whenever she could, she avoided them. She believed in luck and sincerely thought that nothing bad ever befalls you if you're lucky.

In the autumn of 1948, aged four, I started nursery school at the Lycée Français in Heliopolis as my folks decided to give me a French education. France was still a colonizing power in the late forties and a country to be reckoned with. It was the land of culture, human rights, "savoir vivre" and the language of the Egyptian *Khedives*. France had had a strong grip on Egypt since the times of the Second Empire (which ended in 1870 with the defeat of France in its war with Prussia), and the building of the Suez Canal. France's obsession with Egypt dates back to Napoleon Bonaparte's invasion of the country in 1798. It was then that Egypt's ancient culture and its pharaoh's secrets were unveiled to the world through scientists and pundits who accompanied the military expedition. Louis-Napoleon III, his Empress Eugenie and the *Khedive* Ismail were friends. The Emperor surrendered to the Prussians in 1870, while Egypt went bankrupt and couldn't pay back its international loans. The *Khedive* Ismail fled into exile and the country fell into the hands of the British who were after their pound of flesh.

French was considered by the upper Egyptian classes as a "must" a language to be spoken amongst friends even in preference to their native Arabic. They liked to introduce random Arabic words in their French conversations to reflect an attitude, a mood, a state of mind, or simply as a snobbish sign of sophistication.

My first months at school were scary. I knew only Spanish and was anguished and frightened all the time, unable to understand conversations in French and Arabic. It was a traumatic experience and I frequently cried in class. At the request of the *proviseur* (headmaster), my mother came to comfort me during morning breaks. She also spoke only Spanish, but soon caught up, and learned Arabic and French at conversational level. Later, and simultaneously with French and English, I learned the Arabic alphabet which I didn't find difficult. Everything is easy for children. It's a pity that a child's golden learning years are often wasted because of a lack of interest and concentration.

I am left-handed which wasn't considered normal in those days. Therefore, mother compelled me to use my right hand for eating and writing. I am still half left-handed and legged for sport, games and manual work, and the left side of my body is much stronger than the right. I sometimes wonder if, by this unnatural shift, a small chip in my brain could have been damaged or altered, thereby changing forever my character and my abilities. At school I learned quickly and at seven I managed to communicate in three languages.

My Aunt Marisa came to Cairo for the first time in 1949 and met a young man, a Greek neighbour called Stavros. They rode camels, climbed to the top of the great pyramid of Cheops, and took me for long drives in Stavro's car on the desert road that links Cairo and Alexandria. He never drove the car on a full tank. I sat on the back seat behind the driver and while they talked, flirted and laughed (Stavros spoke a little Italian and was very expressive with his hands, which was good enough for my aunt who spoke only Spanish), I watched the needle on the petrol gauge with great attention as it slowly moved towards "empty". I was terribly worried that the car would run out of fuel and we would be stranded for ages in the middle of the empty desert.

In 1950, my father was appointed Headmaster of a junior high-school in the town of Luxor in southern Egypt where we lived for two years. Daddy went ahead of us and a week later Mom and I joined him, travelling by night train the more than seven hundred kilometres from Cairo to Luxor. It was very hot in late September and the *Wagon-lit* coaches were not air-conditioned. Our two-berth cabin comprised a small wash-basin and a tiny ventilator fixed on the partition wall, which did its best to keep us reasonably cool during our long, shaky and almost sleepless night.

Mom told me that on a very hot August night an elderly Englishman travelling that same route and yearning for a touch of cool air brought aboard the train a large block of ice, which he placed facing the ventilator. Then he undressed, lay down stark naked, and drifted off into what was to become his big sleep. The following morning, as he didn't answer the knock-knock-wake-up call on the door, the guard broke in and found him dead and stiff. He had probably died of a heart attack or stroke and not from a blast of cold air. I don't know if this story is true or not. Mother maybe told it to cheer me up over the lack of air conditioning, or maybe she read it in the gossip column of the *Journal d'Egypte,* the sixteen-page French newspaper printed locally for Egypt's foreign community; we made this same journey more than once but I only recall this first one probably because of the dead Englishman.

There was no Lycée Français in Luxor and the only option was an Italian convent school which taught in both Italian and French. I was six years old and not yet into my primary education.

In the early fifties Luxor was not the booming and massive tourist destination it is today. It was a small, muddy, smelly village. Donkeys and *gamoosa* (Egyptian water buffalo used for milk and meat) roamed the streets freely and the sweet smell of dung permanently perfumed the air.

At the time Luxor only attracted archaeologists hunting for mummies and very old, rich Europeans and Americans seeking the warmth of a winter sun and the hot and dry desert sand into which they dipped their weary old bones as a relief for their rheumatism and other curses of old age. The late Agha Khan enjoyed those surroundings so much that he asked to be buried in Aswan. A marble mausoleum indicates the site of his grave.

Sometimes I rode a small jackass led by a *fellah* who held the bridle. Once the man lost control of his animal; it started to kick and stubbornly insisted on jumping a narrow ditch but I held my seat firmly and wasn't thrown.

We shared a large apartment with a school teacher and his family, who kept their side of the house busy with poultry that defecated all over the place. It was chicken stink and shit everywhere and you had to be careful when sitting on the sofa as the birds usually chose that soft spot to lay their morning eggs. The woman slaughtered the hens and roosters in the bathroom or the kitchen by making a small cut in the throat with a razorblade then holding the bird over the sink until it slowly bled to death. We couldn't put up with this nightmarish coop for long and we soon moved to our own apartment. Nevertheless, my mother astounded me, when the following year just before Christmas, she bought a live turkey. For a few days, the bird roamed the house freely and almost became a pet. Then on Christmas Eve she slaughtered it. It was large and heavy so she had to immobilise it by sitting on top of it. Then she neatly cut its throat with a big kitchen knife and the blood immediately gushed out and filled a large pan. She meant to feed us with the best and turkey was good and expensive. Anyhow, it took guts for a town girl like her to do it and for a six-year-old-boy like me to watch it.

My bedroom room window faced a mosque and I listened time after time to the powerful voice of the Muezzin calling the faithful to prayer from the minaret. The call is like a melody, with varied ups and downs and nuances covering unsuspected musical scales. That man was good at his work and it was from him that I first learned how to modulate my voice and croon a song. Later, the King (Elvis) and the Chairman of the Board (Sinatra) took over my musical education. A good Muezzin needs a strong voice and a fine ear. Only one out of fifty Muezzins is good enough and reaches the summit of his skill though it's easier today with modern sound systems. Today, however, the streets of Cairo have become so noisy and stressful because of the thousands of different cries launched at the same time that the authorities have decided to unify them: The best of the muezzins will record the cries which will be broadcast electronically and simultaneously five times a day by all Cairo mosques.

While she waited for me to come out of school, my mother chatted with the Italian nuns about the dreadful conditions of rural Egypt, of its ancestral diseases like trachoma and bilharzia, on how dirty and backward it all was, and how things never changed after more than five thousand years of poverty and bondage. The wealthy *fellaheen* (and there were quite a few) chose to live in frightful hygienic conditions while their wives wore 24-carat gold jewellery. Men nurtured their brains between their legs fathering, with four or more wives, packs of children who were brought up in the same conditions as their beloved *gamoosa* (or worse) without schooling, sanitation or hope for the future and for the unique purpose of helping in the fields. The true population of Egypt is never known. In order to avoid losing their sons to military service for three whole years, the peasants lie to the officials from the statistics bureau about how many male children they have.

One day, while I patiently waited for my mother to end her daily conversation and take me home, the Mother Superior said something I will never forgot. She said that Egypt was a beautiful country like a paradise on earth, with a warm climate and a generous land. The problem she said was the natives, who were dirty and lazy and good for nothing. They should therefore be eliminated and replaced with a better breed. We were shocked and puzzled to hear a nun make such a bold and pitiless statement.

Many years later in Spain, my mother quoted the nun from decades back when she witnessed in Spain many of the flaws she had observed in Egypt such: envy, laziness, irresponsibility and littering. She dreamed of wiping out the whole bloody Spanish race and bringing in a new one, although she knew (but didn't acknowledge) that the major problem lies not in countries or races but in mankind itself.

At school, I befriended two lovely twin girls, the daughters of an Egyptian archaeologist, who drove a World War Two jeep and lived in the desert in a house on the outskirts of Luxor. I was invited to one of their birthday parties but I couldn't attend as we didn't have a car as almost no-one did in those days.

The Luxor Winter Palace Hotel, surrounded by lush gardens and water fountains, was a must for the rich and old cosmopolitan high society. The "crème de la crème" clientele spent many of the winter months there. The hotel had a cinema on the ground floor that was also a tea-room where we could watch movies while enjoying coffee, tea, cakes and cookies, served by elegant, uniformed black *suffragis*. The gardens were my favourite playground.

Fresh from a western in the movie-house, I would run out holding my six-shooter and scream my way around trying to emulate the feats of the cowboy stars I had just watched on the screen, like Roy Rodgers and Gene Autry.

The Ferial was a popular low-grade cinema we seldom visited unless it showed a film I very much wanted to see. Whenever we attended that cinema, we booked a private box in the gallery and were rushed swiftly through the back entrance and up a flight of narrow stairs by the usher. Before the lights went out we watched the populace that had invaded the stalls below dressed up in their *galabiya* (a street robe wore by fellaheen and lower classes), whistling, talking, arguing, eating *leb*, (sunflower seeds) and spitting the shells onto the floor. They also spat spreading out their spittle with the sole of their shoes to erase the traces of their misbehaviour.

This practice, I mean spitting on the pavement, not spreading the spittle, is still pursued by some segments of Spanish society not yet purged from eight centuries of Arab domination. (Our Chinese immigrants also spit like machine guns and thus must feel at ease amongst us). We didn't often attend the Ferial and *Sinbad the Sailor* was the only film I remember viewing there.

We went to the Temples of Abu Simbel, Karnak and other monuments in Luxor and Aswan. They all looked the same: a monotonous display of hieroglyphics carved on huge stones artfully piled on each other as a tribute to the glory of rulers and Gods, as glory is only for the rich, the powerful and the talented.

What will remain of us when we are gone: the Empire State building the Eiffel tower or the good old Roman Coliseum? Probably the colourful McDonald arch which is what we stand for.

When archaeologists discovered the tombs of the pharaohs the graves had already been "discovered", desecrated and looted for hundreds of years. The brigands took the goodies and left the stones for our bewilderment. An archaeologist friend of my father often accompanied us on these excursions and while they talked mummies, old stones and the latest discoveries, I played with the silvery, finger-shaped, powerful flashlight the man used to inspect dark galleries inside pyramids and which I fancied very much. I kept it in my hand for as long as I could and hid it in my pocket just in case he would forget about or give it to me, which he never did.

We spent our summer holidays in Alexandria, and that's when I got the first glimpse of the town we would soon move to. On our first trip we stayed with my uncle Ali Bey and his two sisters; their sea-front apartment along the *Corniche* faced the well-known beach of *Sidi-Bishr.* My elder aunts worshipped my father as the kid brother they brought up as their own son. They were kind and attentive but due to communication problems mother never familiarized or talked much with them.

She disregarded most of the Egyptian cuisine, heavy on *samna,* the fat used in Egypt for cooking. She was a very good cook and at times used the family kitchen to prepare some Spanish delicacy with Italian olive oil. My mother never "really" liked Egypt where she arrived when she was thirty years old. She enjoyed the weather, the beaches, the cosmopolitan atmosphere and the kindness and humility of the people who served her, but, unlike other foreigners settled there for generations, she didn't love the country.

For most foreigners born and bred in Egypt it was hell on earth when they later departed into exile and lost the many advantages they enjoyed such as a huge income, an assortment of servants, large downtown sumptuously furnished apartments, houses on the beach, chauffeured cars and an easy, carefree life. They left Alexandria and dragged their weeping hearts to the four corners of the earth where they found themselves cooped up in sixty square metre flats and listening under the Paris drizzle to the sad laments of French singer Charles Aznavour, when they were used to listening to him on the beaches of Montazah, Stanley and San Stefano.

The month of *Ramadan* (the moveable Muslim fast) caught up with us in July, during our first summer in Alexandria. My father only fasted with the rest of the family for appearance sake and drank water during the day when no-one was around. The food was cooked by the maid hours before it was eaten and laid on the dining-room table awaiting the sunset and the thunder of the cannon announcing that fasting was over for the day. As the eldest son and head of the family my uncle Ali Bey sat at the head of the well-laid table before the rest of the family did, and checked that all was correct while playing with the tips of his upright waxed Turkish moustache. Minutes before sunset, he tied his napkin round his neck and everyone patiently waited for the boom of the cannon releasing the fasters from hunger and thirst. Then the feast began!

The food consisted of a variety of dishes like mutton, veal, fish, pasta, salads and other local delicacies such as stuffed grape-leaves and for dessert very sweet cakes. For mother and me, it was dinner-time and so we joined the others even though we never ate much in the evenings. For the fasters, it was the only meal of the day, after fifteen hard hours without any food or water. Ramadan is very tough in the summertime because of the heat and the long endless days of unrelenting thirst. The next morning, before dawn and twenty minutes before the cannon was fired again to mark a new fasting day, they all woke up and ate and drank for the last time before the following evening.

My second cousin, the son of my cousin Captain Fuad, was my age to the day. He would come to the house escorted by his aunt (good thighs Fifi) and join us on the beach. At five-years old my Arabic must have been quite understandable as we encountered no communication problem while we built our sandcastles with our shovels.

The following summer, we settled for more privacy and rented our own little villa with a garden, approximately one kilometre from the sea. My aunt Marisa, who was visiting us again, stayed for one month in Alexandria.

The episode I most vividly remember from that summer was that incident when I swapped with a boy my age, and for a bottle of Pepsi, a beautiful, red toy racing-car I had received for my birthday. What was wrong with me? Was I so desperate for a cold refreshing drink? Were those pleasures forbidden at home? I guess they were. My parents were not very keen on spending money on those little pleasures which they considered as useless, unhealthy whims. Shortly after I had drunk my Pepsi I missed my toy and was also afraid that my mischief would soon be discovered. I told my father who rushed outside, paid the boy for his Pepsi and recovered my car. His eyes were angry and wild with disbelief. What a stupid son I have, he must have thought. Is he another imbecile anyone can con? For a moment I thought he was going to strike me but he calmed down and told me not to do it again.

My cousin Fuad, his sister Fifi and a friend of the family drawn in by my aunt's beauty took us for drives in Fuad's grand American, automatic black car, on the long and winding *Corniche* and to some of the famous pastry shops like Délices, Trianon or Atheneos, in downtown Alexandria close to Ramleh Station tram terminal.

Two of Délices most tasty cakes were the creamy Palermo and the chocolate *mille feuilles*. Two years later when we moved to Alexandria I bought these at the school canteen.

The Lycée Français canteen crowned by a small faded, worn-out canopy was located in the playground At the far end of the main building next to the bookshop where we bought books and stationery. The canteen only opened at ten o'clock for the fifteen minutes daily recess and sold soft drinks, sandwiches, candy and cakes from *Délices*. It was operated single-handed by a man who tried his best to attend in such a short time to the avalanche of students who stampeded towards the shop as soon as they heard the courtyard bell releasing us from our duties. I always rushed outside as quickly as I could but every time I reached the canteen I had to stand behind a double or a triple row of the agitated, hollering and waving madmen who had preceded me. I jumped higher and faster than the rest, shouting my order and keeping up, like a fist of fury, the hand holding the money. When my turn finally came it was sheer luck if one of my favourite cakes was still available. The secret of success was to be the tallest of the pack—which I was not—or to yell louder than the rest, which I could not.

CHAPTER NINE

In the autumn, before classes started, we returned to Luxor. One year later we settled for good in Alexandria. My father had been appointed Head Master of a secondary school in the town of Damanhur situated in the Nile Delta barely thirty minutes by train from Alexandria. He surely became one of the first commuters in Egypt as he travelled daily on the first passenger train on the Africa continent, the Express from Cairo to Alexandria we called "the diesel". The train covered the two hundred and twenty plus kilometres between the two cities in less than three hours. The project was conceived carried out and inaugurated in the second half of the nineteenth century.

We took an apartment in the residential district of Victoria where stood the renowned English School Victoria College, *alma mater* to many famous, rich and powerful people like the late King Hussein of Jordan and the financier Khashoggi. Victoria was also the end of line for the tram which covered the distance to *Ramleh* terminal station located in downtown Alexandria in less than forty minutes.

The Lycée Français at Chatby Station was thirty minutes from home by tram. We got off one stop before at Camp-César, which was a more lively location and walked the short five minutes distance between the two stations. The tram network in Alexandria is "the" main public transportation system. It runs inland less than one kilometre from the sea covering commercial and residential areas.

My father rented an apartment in the district of Victoria because his best friend Abdel Kader Baraka lived there with his wife Lula in a large house with a back garden, one hundred metres away from where we rented our flat. He felt that it would be safer for us to have the Barakas close at hand when he was away.

The Barakas had no children and "adopted" me on the spot. They were kind, generous and hospitable. My mother called them *Pepo* and *Pepa* because they reminded her of two characters in some children's magazine she had read in Spain. The couple spoke French and they got along beautifully as she learned the language and spoke it with certain easiness.

Abdel Kader was five years older than my father. He was a civil servant and worked in the Port of Alexandria as a Customs supervisor. The couple kept an old Nubian (southern Egypt, bordering with the Sudan) cook who had been Baraka's nanny and a Sudanese boy of twelve named *Osman* who was being trained as a *suffragi*.

Lula firmly believed in a popular superstition which guaranteed that if a woman wished to get pregnant all she had to do was watch the reflection of a full moon on a child's face. My mother was of course incredulous but she agreed to the experiment just to please her. The trick was performed while I stood still facing the moon for thirty minutes and for three consecutive full moons; but the miracle never worked out and they remained childless.

Baraka displayed on his upper lip a ridiculously small moustache, no larger than a fly. He laughed heartily each time I tried to grab it and asked him what use was that *petite salété* (little piece of dirt) under his nose.

We were a family of just three but we took on a full-time maid who lived in; mother cooked, while the maid cleaned the house. Upper-class Egyptians and khawagat often had more than one servant. Lula convinced my mother that the household of a senior teacher and headmaster should have at least one maid. Otherwise *ce ne serait pas comme il faut* (it wouldn't be respectable for appearances sake). We also adopted a dog and until my final departure from Alexandria we kept on taking dog after dog, all of uncertain breeds. We were rather unlucky and many of them died on us. Our Victoria dog died tragically when he was a year or so old. One winter night, he started to howl to the death and vomit green stuff. My father was away. He had been re-assigned somewhere else quite far from Alexandria and he only came home at week-ends. At midnight I rushed out and called on our friend Baraka; I woke him up and dragged him out of bed. He rushed behind me in his pyjamas and slippers. We did all we could to save it but at dawn and in spite of our efforts he was dead after a terrible agony. It clearly looked like a case of mischievous poisoning and we immediately suspected the maid for the apparent disregard for animals she had showed on many occasions. But we had no proof to back our suspicions. Arabs generally do not like dogs which they consider impure, dirty and useless; stray dogs are frequently and pitilessly stoned by children.

We threw the dead body on a wasteland not far from home. One week later, and out of a morbid curiosity or weird fascination for death or simply because I was already thinking more than I should have about the ephemeral and the uselessness of life, I revisited the burial ground, a well-ventilated space. The stench was bearable. The sun had got very quickly to the carcass. It was almost rotten and gone except the eye cavities, the wrinkled brown hide and the white teeth twisted in a sad goodbye grin. Nature's worst curse on man is to let him know that someday he has to die and that life is not for keeps. It's like constant harassment which ends with . . . death and . . . . relief. It is our one and only punishment as well as our purgatory. Man is the only animal who is conscious of his own death on a daily basis. No other living being is subject to such a torture. Other animals are only conscious of death when their instinct for preservation is triggered moments before the end.

Each morning, at seven-thirty, we took the tram from Victoria to Camp-César. As I mentioned, the Lycée was located at Chatby but we preferred to walk the straight street between the two stops, which bordered the tracks and led to the school. It also saved us the effort of climbing the two dozen steps of Chatby Station which was below street level. It was still early but the many shops such as the second-hand bookshop (where I sold my old school books and got myself some extra cash), the grocer's, the juice-store, the barber's, the falafel restaurant and others, had been open since first light and were ready for business.

Classes started at precisely eight o'clock from Monday to Saturday. My mother took that same ride on the tram four times a day. After she safely left me in school, she returned home to cook lunch and then came back at one-thirty to pick me up. There were no afternoon classes and I had lots of time to spare for homework and leisure.

On Saturday evenings we went to the movies, to one of the two double-feature cinemas, the Odeon and the Gaité, the former in Camp-César and the latter near the preceding tram station of Ibrahimieh.

One evening, on our way back from the Odeon my stomach turned upside-down and I puked in the tram. My mother blamed the cone of roasted peanuts I avidly devoured during the interval for my misery, but I was sure it was because of *Quo Vadis* the epic film we had just watched in which the Romans feed groups of Christians to starving lions which devour them like candy. I wondered why the audience laughed and hissed and tapped their feet each time Emperor Nero (Peter Ustinov) appeared on the screen. I was later told that Egyptian State propaganda led the people to believe that the corpulent Nero, recipient of all vices including debauchery, was an exact replica of the infamous, fat ex-King Farouk who had been recently dethroned and sent into exile by the "free" Officers of the 1952 Revolution.

My pretty and knowledgeable neighbour Farida lived in a house with a garden just across from the building where we lived. She was probably given that name as homage to the Egyptian Royal Family. She was born in the early forties when King Farouk was still married to his first Queen whom he renamed Farida because of his obsession for the "F" word (don't laugh) which he considered lucky; then, the names of the members of his family started with "F". During those years, new-born girls in Egypt were frequently named Faika, Fawziya or Fairuz following the king's tradition.

Farida's mother was a tall, statuesque red-haired German. She was a teacher at the Berlitz School of Languages in downtown Alexandria. Her father, an Egyptian of Turkish descent didn't live with his family. I only saw him once around the house and she never talked about him, so I rightly guessed that her parents were divorced. Her German grandparents also lived in the family house and looked after her while her mother was at work. She was one year older than me, attended the German School and looked like movie actress Marian Carr, the pretty aerialist in the film *Ring of Fear*. In the evenings after school we played in her garden, which was presided by a huge mango tree always loaded with the delicious, incomparable fruit. The smell of jasmine was overwhelming especially during those warm summer nights I passed by her house, when walking my dog.

Farida and I played games such as "doctors and nurses" and "Anthony and Cleopatra". When she slightly spread her legs in the middle of a game, I could see her wispy, puppy fluff through her little *culotte* (panties) and wondered why I had still none. Like all little girls, she was older than her years with a malicious, irresistible twinkle in her eyes. She reckoned that I was a good playmate and that she liked my eyes which she considered very Spanish. But if she had had to choose between the two friends she had, she would undoubtedly go for the riches of her next-door neighbour, who was six years older than her, lived in a palace and was the son and heir of the very wealthy Calza Bey.

The boy owned a new shining red Italian *Vespa* scooter (the *Vespa* and the *Lambretta* were the favourite two-wheel vehicles of the well-off youngsters in Alexandria), and could take her to downtown cinemas and the exclusive beaches of Stanley and San Stefano. As far as I was concerned it was a hopeless one-side romance. At ten, she was already a full grown bitch.

I was too young to drive a motor vehicle and my father never had the means to buy me one. The Spanish bicycle I brought from Madrid had been discarded when I became too big for it. Anyway I knew that Farida was too sophisticated to sit on the handlebars as my first girl Barbara did years ago in Cairo when we were both four years old.

We often picked mangos from the tree and ate them on the spot. That garden was a haven-like paradise minus the apple tree. However, we never played "Adam and Eve";

it was too obvious and we were too shy to play our parts as required in the original script. One day, in the course of one of our games, she maliciously threw sand into my eyes and in return I kicked her arse. Our friendship ended there and then, and we never talked to each other again. A few months later we moved to an apartment in the district of Camp-César and Farida and I definitely lost touch. I was eight years old when we first met, but I haven't forgotten her, though more than half a century has elapsed since our childhood.

Years later, I kept haunting my old Victoria neighbourhood, far away from the beaten track of my district, just for the pleasure of a tram-journey or a ride on a rented bicycle, singing Neil Sedaka's hits, *Little Devil, Happy Birthday Sweet Sixteen and Stairway to Heaven*—to myself. Those teenage songs suited Farida beautifully and had been creeping inside me for years; wherever I went, those melodies always brought her to my mind.

On those Victoria jaunts, I watched her house from a reasonable distance trying to catch a glimpse of her. Once, I caught up with Farida when she was about to mount a *Vespa*, which I suspected belonged to that guy Calza she boasted about when we were children. I approached and asked her if she recognised her buddy from the old days. She looked at me and shook her head, but as if she didn't mean it. Then she swiftly got on her friend's *Vespa* and off they went.

The year before I left Alexandria and while still at the Lycée, I saw her more than once sitting by the window in her German school bus as it slowly passed in front of our building. She had become an exquisite, beautiful young woman. I never waved at her or tried to catch her attention. If she'd recognized me, she probably would have snobbishly ignored me, a much worse blow for my ego than not being recalled at all.

There is a scene in *Citizen Kane*, when one of the characters, a Mr Bernstein, an old man in a retirement home, confesses to a reporter that decades ago he saw a girl on the ferry from Manhattan to Staten Island. She was wearing a white dress and a matching hat and, although he saw her just for a few moments, a month hasn't gone by since that he hadn't thought of her.

Opposite our Victoria building, there was a *caracol* or *shorta* (a police station) where suspects were brought in for identification and interrogation. The word *shorta* meaning police probably comes from the English word "shorts" related to the short pants usually worn by the British personnel in warm or tropical countries.

From our window we had a full view of the police station's backyard. Twice or three times a week, fifteen or twenty detainees dressed in their *galabiya* were brought into the yard. They squatted in a long line, their arms on their knees, their bottoms almost touching the ground. Then the *shaweesh* (policemen) released a trained German shepherd dog on the detainees. The dog strolled up and down the line; he came and went, restlessly sniffing his way and trying to detect amongst the men the reek of the token he had previously smelled. When he had sorted out who the suspect was, he gave a bark and sprang towards him, grabbing the man's *galabiya* or viciously biting an arm or leg. The *shaweesh* then took the dog away and led the suspect into the main building for proper questioning. We could hear the screams and the denials and pleas for mercy from the man under interrogation. After a while it was all over as a full confession had surely been obtained.

My mother never felt sorry for those or any other detainees. She reckoned they were criminals and had to be severely punished. During the Spanish Civil War she had endured more than her share of criminality and murder. "The difference between Egyptian and European interrogation methods" (she possibly meant Spanish methods in the post-war years), she told me, "Is that here it's carried out almost in the open for everyone to listen and learn, and not behind closed doors as in civilised countries". She was a tough cookie and had witnessed many dreadful deeds during the war performed by both the Republicans and Fascists alike. She came from a well-off middle-class family and was therefore rabidly anti-Republican and anti-communist.

She and her sister spent most of the Civil War with relatives in the food-abundant, agricultural coastal town of Valencia in eastern Spain, held by the Republican army. Before the end of the war they returned to Madrid, because of the sexual harassment she had to endure from her step-uncle Don José (her aunt's husband). She confided in her aunt who didn't believe her. She called her an ungrateful bitch and a liar and immediately confronted her with the husband who denied everything. The wife of course "believed" him and both sisters were kicked out of the family home. With the help of a cousin who was a Republican lieutenant, they were smuggled across the war lines in a truck hidden amid dozens of sacks of potatoes. These were being sent from Valencia to feed the hungry population of Madrid then surrounded by Franco's troops, ready for the final assault and the end of the war.

Aside from burning churches man's favourite sport in Republican-held towns was the hunt for hidden priests and nuns for immediate execution with a bullet in the neck.

Although reprehensible, such actions were comprehensible in a chaotic scenario and reflected the true nature of Man in extreme and lawless circumstances. The burning of churches and the persecution of the clergy was just revenge against the gruesome, pitiless grip that Church, Monarchy and riches, former rulers of the country, had exerted for centuries on the dispossessed. The oppressed masses were now taking their due.

At the beginning of the war and before the departure of her family to Valencia, Don José, a famous, wealthy lawyer tried to save a young priest and a nun from death, hiding them in his Madrid apartment. The nun posed as a housemaid and the priest as a valet. One day, while my mother was visiting, the militia came to the house looking for churchmen or any other goodies they could lay their hands on. The nun acted her role, held her ground and even flirted with the men, while the priest, paralysed with fear, pissed in his pants and confessed who he really was. They took him away and shot him the following day.

My father looked tough, but was mild. He was meek and grouchy and rough at times but he was just a lamb in a wolf's coat. He was not apparently concerned and never talked about the sinister and perilous path his country was taking after the 1952 revolution.

Patriotism is a refuge for scoundrels and what the "free and patriotic officers" first did after their "coup" was to cancel freedom. The *Mokhabarat* (a word meaning in Arabic those who gather information i.e. State Police) were everywhere and in later years I even came to fear one of my Egyptian classmates I believed too patriotic to be trusted. He befriended on the beaches of *Maamura* (a resort visited mostly by high-ranking officers and their families), the sons of the brass, and I came to think he was a snitch or would be one.

On my trip to Alexandria in November 2010, I was informed that the combined forces of the police and the secret services amounted to one million five hundred thousand agents for a population of eighty-five millions. That's one informer for every fifty-six citizens.

Nasser was a patriot but his ferocious Egyptian nationalism and his misplaced Pan—Arabian dreams got the best of him. He chewed more than he could swallow and finally choked on his ambitions. The "socialist" regime he imposed on the country was opposed to the historical mentality and way of life of the Egyptians. It also cost him the financial support of the United States which thought he was a "fucking commie" which he was not. He also failed to consider the realities of the Arab countries. He thought in his delusion that he could be not only Egypt's *Raïs*, but also the lighthouse and moral leader of all Arabs with Egypt being the guardian of history, tradition, literature, movies and music exported to the whole Arab world from Morocco to Yemen.

His bloodless revolution which targeted the wretched masses was meant to change things for the better but it didn't. If anything it changed them for worse. He locked himself in a bubble of pride and ignorance, ignoring or waving aside the harsh realities of the Arab mentality: a strong sense of individualism, a lack of unity and cooperation, and a deep distrust for one another spiced with religious differences, blood feuds, macho attitudes and illiteracy. The British knew those flaws only too well and cleverly used them to achieve their aims in Arab countries during the colonial years. The road to democracy is full of stumbling blocks. For law and order to prevail, corruption and injustice have to be accepted and swept under the carpet. These countries will continue to be ruled by severe, traditional monarchies or by strong, harsh dictatorships. Nasser's goal to unite the Arab nations and to motivate the Egyptian crowds took shape in his constant obsession with Israel as the common enemy and source of all evils and referred to in his speeches as "a thorn in the heart of Arab countries".

My aunt thought him very handsome, not lacking in panache, with eyes as bright and burning as two "black glowing embers". It's true that he had a strong personality and a special magnetism which drew the rest of the Arab leaders into his sphere of influence.

"Israel, a thorn in the heart of the Arab countries" topic was the theme I chose from the three offered and which I developed into a four-hundred-word essay for my final Arabic examination in June 1963. The other two subjects were "Egypt's industrial revolution" and "the Aswan High Dam" which was being financed and built by Russia's Nikita Khrushchev (or *kharchuv* as he was nick-named, meaning "artichoke" in Arabic). I was very imaginative on this issue and passed my exam, after writing a lot of rubbish about how the Jewish "thorn" deeply pierced the poor Arab hearts. I made a wise decision in choosing this theme. The other two subjects were also "hot" but this one was top of the list and an all-time favourite of the examiners at a time when Nasser was preparing to wage war on Israel.

Nasser was an interloper, a self-proclaimed leader of the Arab world and believed he had the right and the moral obligation to meddle with other countries' internal affairs. His efforts as a defender of the Arab cause shrouded his failure to get Egypt on its feet and to change it into a better and more just society. Maybe he chose the right track and knew what he was doing as the latter is really "an impossible dream".

He sided with Algeria which he financed with money and weapons during their fight for independence and consequently brought upon him the wrath of France. In 1958, he urged Muslim rebels in Lebanon to revolt against the legal government.

In 1962, he sent an Egyptian military expedition to Yemen to back up the Republicans in their fight against the Monarchists who were supported by Saudi Arabia, What he achieved in Yemen after five years of treacherous warfare between opposing "Arab brothers" was the misuse of large amounts of the much-needed cash wasted on ungrateful rascals, who slaughtered Egyptian soldiers in the barber shops of the capital Sanaa by slitting their throats with razors while leaning back on the adjustable chair, waiting for a pleasant shave, their cheeks and chins covered in foam. The poor bastards never knew what had hit them; it was the final smack of Yemeni hospitality.

He also supported the Fidel Castro Regime during the Bay of the Pigs crisis, but I will comment on this later, as my classmates and I played an important role in encouraging and steering large crowds in a street demonstration.

The ungovernable and almost illiterate Egyptian masses loaded with thousands of years of idiosyncrasies and traditions loved and cheered him but also let him down by their indiscipline and indifference. He probably believed that his beloved Arabs were "more like the Germans" and wrongly concluded that he could count on them to receive the same support Hitler had obtained from his masses in 1933 and after. He died in 1970, a defeated has-been giant who had enhanced his image, by trying to motivate his people and foster unachievable global Arab nationalism and unity. The crowds of Egypt rushed in millions to his funeral. They screamed, wept, tore their clothes and in the turmoil were trampled. Many were injured and some died for their dead leader in a very emotional and absurd Egyptian fashion.

The *Aïd al Adha*, (sacrificial day) or the "day of the sheep" as we called it at home, is the day when duty calls every good Muslim to sacrifice a lamb just as Abraham (known in Egypt by his Muslim name Ibrahim) did to save his son following God's mouth to ear instructions. It is a tradition on that day to share the meal with the less fortunate though I doubt if this custom is still in use as there are too many poor and not enough generous rich.

The Baraka's kept the sacrificial lamb in their basement for days before the big event. I visited the miserable, soiled animal, which was constantly fed to keep it fat. The poor lamb reeked like hell as sheep in Egypt do. The stink and strong flavour of the meat is surely related to what they eat and to a lack of hygiene as their coats and fat tails are covered with mud and dung.

On the fatidic day a butcher loaded with an assortment of knives called at six in the morning to proceed with the sacrifice. He tied the lamb's hooves together, lay it down on the sandy floor, then slaughtered and skinned the animal, leaving the bloody fleece to dry and be used later as a rug in the servants' quarters.

Our share of "the sacrifice" was to accept their invitation to lunch. It was a ceremony I dreaded but there was no escape.

To confer a "gourmet touch" to this unique happening it was the custom to roast the lamb's brain in the oven prior to detaching it from the skull like a precious pearl from an oyster-shell.

The table was sumptuously laid in classical Egyptian style with a display of cold dishes including pieces of roast lamb, pasta, a large variety of salads, different types of *homos* (Egyptian salads) and other local delicacies.

We all sat and nibbled and waited for the "piece de resistance". When the brain was well-cooked inside its natural recipient *Mabruka* brought the burned skull from the kitchen on a large tray. The head with the big protruding sad eyes looked like that of John the Baptist in the film *Salome*.

Then Baraka, as lord and master of ceremonies proceeded with the most important and delicate mission of splitting the skull wide-open with a chisel and hammer to liberate its delicious contents. He handled his instruments with the same care and precision any construction worker would, when breaking through a solid, brick wall.

His first efforts were unsuccessful and sometimes in one of those strong blows, the head would sweep off the tray and land on the floor. Finally his tenacity was blessed with success. The skull cracked and the long-expected reward appeared: a beautiful, steaming greyish brain.

My father, a semi-vegetarian who ate meat only on rare occasions, had averted his eyes from the performance. He smiled and politely declined the delicacy. My mother graciously accepted a small piece of cold meat and a plate of *homos* with a green salad. I passed as I always did on these occasions, ate a pear and waited for an early dinner at home. The surgical achievement of our friend Baraka and the rancid odour of the meat displayed on the table acted on me as an antidote and many years passed by before I started to eat and appreciate roast lamb which is a Spanish speciality.

CHAPTER TEN

Summer holidays were long and hot in Alexandria lasting from the middle of June until the end of September. Mom loved the heat and the beach and the sun tan. I did not.

The beach on which we anchored our umbrella was called Mandara, a pebbled shore with hardly any sand, located within reasonable walking distance (one kilometre) from home.

Green, slippery seaweed covered the waterfront rocks making the approach to the sea uncomfortable and a bit hazardous.

I carried the heavy, striped multicoloured umbrella on my shoulder, while Mom handled the wooden, spear-head stick which we planted on the ground amidst the pebbles to hold it. I learned to swim in shallow waters lying on my belly and touching the rocky bottom with my out-stretched arms, while I was carried to and fro at the whim of the mild, lukewarm waves. There was a deep, dark abyss just off the reef, a few metres from were I sprawled, but I never went that way. I wasn't too sure of my swimming abilities and I dreaded falling into it and not being able to swim my way out. It was a bottomless pit filled with troubled waters. I imagined that it was crammed with colourless, blind, mysterious creatures from the very deep where daylight never filtered. I floundered for a long time in shallow waters, until I began to tremble, my body covered with goose pimples and my hands all wrinkled and pale.

At the end of one summer season I felt more confident, took a leap of faith and dived into the abyss. I frenetically crossed it a couple of times, wriggling my arms and legs like a puppy trying to keep afloat.

We lingered on the beach until lunchtime when we folded our umbrella packed our towels and returned home still wearing our wet bathing suits under our clothes, as there were no public showers to wash the salt away. I felt uncomfortable and impatient to get home to the relief of a shower. Mom said that it was good for my health to keep the salt on my body for a while like a salted cod. I never knew if she was joking or if she really meant it.

On our way home, we were sometimes given a lift in an Austin car by a Greek female nurse back from her hospital shift and who lived alone in a green building opposite ours. I heard her ask my mother if she shaved her *petit oiseau*. She knew that my father was Egyptian and that it was custom for Arab men and women to shave their private parts. Women used to remove body hair with a home-made, golden, thick paste called *halawa* (also the name of a sweet), made of sugar and lemon and heated to the right temperature. My mother replied bluntly that she was not a native and that my father was too civilised to care for such matters.

She later learned to make *halawa,* which requires a very special blend of the ingredients and set up her own little business for acquaintances and friends in Madrid. That nurse also gave me shots of penicillin during the seasonal flu epidemics, when my body temperature regularly rose to over 40º C. She disinfected her syringes and needles in boiling water which was the way in those days, but quite useless to prevent AIDS or hepatitis. Fortunately the former was still science fiction but the latter . . . . well, as my mother said one has to be lucky.

The overall feeling of insecurity and fear of danger that haunt people today were unusual then and life was generally more rewarding. Stress and mental depressions were the exception and not the rule, and those suffering from the symptoms were called "unstable" or "sad". There weren't any shrinks or antidepressants to deal with those ailments. Adults seldom died in their prime from cancer, strokes, heart attacks, or of some mysterious, viral disease so frequent nowadays. Children were healthy and allergies were unheard of.

The only exception I knew concerned one of my classmates named Asaad. Diabetic by birth, he was small and underweight and at ten, he started to lose his hair and his sight. His father was a doctor and gave him daily insulin shots. He had to read and write with the help of a magnifying glass and always made it a point of honour not to let the teachers help him in any way, as they knew that he couldn't make it even with the help of the glass.

During our State final examinations, at the end of Junior School, he reacted violently within the limits of his weakness towards one of the supervisors who, unaware of his pride and integrity, tried to help him not only to understand the questions but with the answers as well.

His hobby was to build and launch miniature rockets (it was soon after the Russian Sputnik started the space age) that dashed straight up into the sky, died there and were lost forever, just as it happened to Asaad himself who passed away when he was only twenty-five. I reckon that he finally gave up fighting when his exhausted little body could take no more pain. He was born a sick child, lived for a while and died young. In his own way I suppose he enjoyed his short life for as long as it lasted before returning to nothingness.

Was it worth it? Was it better that he had never been born? I don't know.

When my father walked in the sun which wasn't very often he held a folded newspaper at arm's length over his head to prevent direct, unnecessary exposure, as if he knew then, as we know now of the dangers in store. During Alexandria's cool months and Spanish winters, he wore the dark-blue French beret with the tip on top, to protect his bald pate.

Just like my father, I don't appreciate the sun or the heat either. Those daily summer journeys to the *Mandara* seashore weighed heavily on my body and my spirit as they became too frequent, too boring and too tiresome. I was a strong but skinny kid but the prolonged daily sea bathing, the unrelenting salt on my body and the walks to and fro were getting the best of me. Summer holidays proved to be a repetitive, daily nightmare, more monotonous and tiresome than school itself. Mom remained adamant and refused to listen to my pleas to negotiate about her beloved beach; "Mom knows best" she said, just like a British nanny would, asserting that I would die of boredom if I stayed at home all day long.

I avoided discussing the matter further, but I believed I would be better off in Farida's shadowy Garden of Eden, busy with our provocative games, trying new and lavish ones, learning the facts of life live from the birds and the bees, and eating ripe mangos off the tree. At the end of August I was still looking for a way out, and longing for the month of October to get back to school.

In the evenings when my folks went out, the maid told me stories about *ghouls* (Arab demons), Sultans, Princes, Princesses and wicked Viziers like those in the Arabian Nights. When I listened to her I would stand at my bedroom window from where I could see the back of the building facing ours with its large white wall like a cinema screen. While she was slowly telling her fantastic tales, my imagination shifted her words into a full Technicolor movie, which I mentally projected ten metres across the street on my very own personal screen.

In Egypt, there were very few films barred from under-sixteens. I recall fewer than half-a-dozen such movies: *Summer Place* (because of the cherry business), *Baby Doll* (Carol Baker was over the top when she sucked her thumb in her cot), and *Psycho* considered violent and bloody because of the shower scene. I therefore saw many other films which in other countries were for adult audiences only.

Because of the movies I watched in the fifties, I started to feel an intense attraction for the United States and everything that came from Hollywood. America became to me a mosaic of fairy tales: family houses with manicured gardens and neat driveways, helpful, inquisitive and gossiping neighbours, light-hearted and hard-working delivery boys making their deliveries through unlocked back-doors into state-of-the-art kitchens, pushy little housewives with the word "alimony" stamped on their foreheads, strong, successful short-haired-bull husbands looking forward to fuck the girl next door because the grass is always greener there. Back then, there were no tits or pussy or straight sex or faggots on the screen and the only drugs praised and highly encouraged were cigarettes and plenty of after-hours martinis.

In Egypt, smoking was permitted in the theatres. The perfumed, cancerous blue clouds of smoke blown up in the air over our heads by the viewers mixed with the less hazardous fumes exhaled by the actors smoking on the screen. It was a delight to watch Bogart light a cigarette, inhale deeply and gently exhale through his mouth and nostrils, casting a blue-grey halo which enveloped his face. It was a hard thing to watch for those who were trying to quit the habit, and an inspiration to teenage smokers who were starting to learn the facts of life by breeding their cancer.

We watched westerns, war films, musicals, comedies and light melodramas, featuring tasty blondes, hot brunettes and well-intentioned all-American-antiseptic men with neat haircuts but very little brain to match their imposing looks.

America is obsessed with *The Wizard of Oz* which seems to be for many a solace for every unfulfilled dream of fame, power and wealth. Come back to earth fellows. There is no secret door to break free into a magic fourth dimension.

I loved the soundtracks even more than the films. I cannot always remember the stories of those movies, but I remember the tunes. Sometimes the reason we have such deep, lasting, emotional connections to the movies is the music. The melody is what keeps you tied to a film forever.

My favourite film was *Young at Heart*. I was nine or ten when I saw it and Frank Sinatra became—and still is—my favourite crooner. After the movie came out, I saw some of the songs from the film soundtrack on a 45 R.P.M in a shop-window. But the record was too expensive for our budget and I didn't have a player either, although I would have enjoyed buying it just for the pleasure of starting a collection.

Those rosy Technicolor movies were "coloured free" meaning that blacks were "blacklisted", off limits and only tolerated as distinguished servants to the brass.

The infamous Hollywood real blacklist of actors and writers was also long forgotten.

Globally speaking, cinematography never made it as a major art because films are expensive to make and thus there is the commercial need to please everybody.

Great films have been made though, true masterpieces which are the exception to the rule. Nowadays inspiration and ideas in movies have almost dried out and the only productive "imagination" is that of the special effects and sound.

For the middle-class white American the fifties and early sixties should have been the golden years, arrayed with the solid, all-time values extolled by the "American way of life", except that all those values were phoney and still are. Hypocrisy was and still is the name of the game. "In God We Trust" is the motto printed on American currency. Definitely, God, money and the watchful oval eye of the freemasonry form a perfect trio, walking hand in hand.

My American dream became a more tangible reality when we called on a young couple of Egyptian teachers who were back from California, where they had spent a full year on a scholarship. They spoke with awe of their life there and of the wonderful things they had learned and experienced. They lived in Hollywood next door to Doris Day, who smiled and said hello when she returned from the Studios in the evenings

So it was all true, I thought later. Those fancy screen images haunted me for sometime, like a mirage I couldn't quite believe or grab. As years went by, time kept speeding on, catching up with me, until I got carried away in a merciless ever-accelerating time machine, living misspent, useless days.

Do Americans still believe or have ever believed in the utopian slogan "the pursuit of happiness"? Is it only another article in the Constitution or just part of the built-in hypocrisy? By now they should be disillusioned as they are no longer so young or candid. Have the lessons of time and history smartened up the average John Doe? I don't think so, well at least not yet.

Happiness is non-existent except for a few, fleeting moments which you seize here and there: I call them "short spells of peace of mind". My quest is not to seek happiness but to avoid misfortune. But I'm not bothered or surprised when unhappiness comes my way: it's a part of the same game to have your share of everything.

Mom discovered one day that the infamous maid whom we suspected of poisoning our dog was developing a large belly—not in accordance with her unmarried state. As my father wasn't home much and I was too young to be held responsible for such a scandal, she was fired on the spot; it was the end of live-in maids.

In the evenings, my mother and I took walks along a street lined with trees which blossomed with small scarlet red balls in spring. As we strolled along we played a game we called "professions". Mom pointed at an almost fruitless tree and said, "This one must be a teacher; see how poor it is". The next one's boughs were heavy with the red fruit. "Ho ho, this one, on the other hand, must be a physician an engineer or a businessman" she nodded, "See how wealthy it is".

She had nothing against my father's profession, but she missed the ready cash other people seemed to enjoy. She never understood my father well and thus missed a very important point concerning his character: Dad was an intellectual and intellectuals are seldom ambitious as far as the riches of the world are concerned, especially if they live in developing countries. Furthermore Egyptian school teachers never reached well-compensated social or professional heights. What vexed my mother most was not the extra, sometimes necessary cash my father could not provide, but his lack of spirit and aspirations. He never shared an idea or an opinion. If we spoke our mind on any given subject that at times concerned him, he sulked, adopted the attitude of a martyr about to be sacrificed, and answered that we were always trying to diminish and insult him.

My mother was not a big spender (she couldn't be) but she didn't respect money either. She never worked for it and maybe she thought it grew on trees like those little red balls.

She always bought the best food in the market and was probably right because in those days there was little else to buy. She dressed impeccably and behaved as if she were a millionairess, which was something good for her ego. My father knew she had a hole in the palm of her hand and implanted a system for the safe distribution of the family income.

On the first day of each month, as soon as father was back from the Misr Bank (*Misr* or *Masr* is the Arabic name for Egypt) where he kept an account and cashed his salary, we sat expectantly around the living-room table.

He divided the bank-notes into small piles to cover each part of our fixed monthly expenses: the house rent, school fees, food, entertainment, etc . . . . Once the distribution was completed, there wasn't much left for any unforeseen extras. However, I felt content as there was always a small amount for the movies and for my little weaknesses such as the cakes from *Délices*, the *fool* (beans) sandwich with boiled egg; the pasta stuffed with chopped meat from the downtown restaurant *Lourantos*, and my weekly French magazines, *Tintin* and the *Journal de Mickey*. All these "excesses" put together amounted to no more than three Egyptian Pounds, which, at today's exchange rate would be forty euro cents.

In 1963 and just before retiring, my father was drawing a monthly salary of fifty Egyptian Pounds per month i.e. seven euro. It's a ridiculous sum by today's standards, but in 1963 when the Beatles were starting their vertiginous rise to fame and fortune and I was still a nineteen-year-old, half baked, pimpled cookie, his salary was quite respectable and paid for our needs. The Lycée Français was expensive, but the fees were subsidised at seventy-five percent as my father belonged to the teaching profession.

Like most people, we had no car, telephone, washing machine, refrigerator (just an ice-box), water-heater, or holidays abroad.

The man who provided us with our daily supply of ice was the *bawab* of a building down the street. He was a black Nubian giant and, punctually each morning before noon, he delivered our order of half-a-bar which he carried wrapped in a brown sack on his broad shoulders. As he walked the ice melted and his route could be detected by the trail of water he left behind.

The milkman came by late in the evening, riding a heavy black bicycle laden with two twenty-litre tin churns of *gamoosa* milk, topped with half-an-inch of yellowish cream. While he pedalled, he held one end of his *galabiya* between his teeth to prevent it from being caught between the chain and the pedals. Mom always boiled our litre in an aluminium pan and let the milk rise and fall three consecutive times, convinced that no tuberculosis bacillus could survive such a treatment.

Only the privileged few could afford the luxuries and the comforts of modern appliances like those we saw in the movies; they were scarce anyway. My cousin "good thighs" Fifi bought a huge refrigerator with a freezer. She didn't use it for what it was meant for, but placed it unplugged in a corner of the drawing-room to be displayed as an expensive, white, work of art. The doors were left ajar and, the top crowned with a flower pot. Whenever we called on her, I gazed at it in awe and imagined all the ice-cream that could be manufactured inside that large wasted freezer.

Travelling to Europe or Lebanon, the favourite summer destinations, was the prerogative of only the very wealthy. Anyhow, who needed Paris, London or Rome—you could hardly imagine them, least of all hope to see them, when your illusions and fun were here at home, within the spectrum of the simple entertainments in our daily lives?

Television sets were starting to pop-up but that never concerned us, as the one and only available channel was in Arabic. However, we had a Philips radio; we tuned into Radio Montecarlo or Radio France International for world news and good music. French singer Charles Aznavour was one of our favourites and, because of his shy, broken voice and the content of his songs, mother compared his singing to the melancholy lament of a cuckolded, compliant husband.

Some people kept their radios well covered up to prevent the cockroaches always looking for the warmth of the valves, from getting inside and eating up the slender threads. These were large receivers made of dark oak with mother-of-pearl buttons and one front loudspeaker covered with brown fabric.

We also listened to Cairo stations which regularly broadcast American and French music. I once caught an interview in Arabic with Dalida, an Italian-Egyptian singer living in Paris, who was revisiting her hometown Cairo. Her new Egyptian fans welcomed her as *bent al balad* (daughter of the country) months after her big success in France with the hit song *Bambino*.

The hot water required for the weekly home-laundry session was heated in a fifteen—litre tin drum laid on top of a red-hot Primus burner (British-made contraption, fuelled with cheap petrol that was very popular in Egypt for kitchen purposes), placed on the bathroom floor. The maid sat on a small wooden stool her legs spread out and mixed the hot and cold water. She then washed the clothes with a large piece of green soap, rinsed them carefully and hung them to dry on the large terrace on top of the building which was used by all the neighbours for the same purpose.

In the summer, we had cold showers as the water was lukewarm and pleasant. In the winter months, however, the drum was lifted into the bathtub, the hot water conveniently mixed with the cold from the tap. Hot water was always heated on the Primus. We had a gas stove in the kitchen but the blue bottles of Butane were expensive and used for cooking only. Winters were mild and our gas-heater on wheels was sufficient to warm up the hall, living-room and both bedrooms.

That Arthur Miller look. Father in the 30s (Cairo)

02

My "tarbooshed" daddy. (Tetuán 1944)

Aunt Marisa and friend on top of the world
(the Cheops pyramid 1949)

04

Riding high (Cairo 1949)

05

Father and son (Luxor 1951)

06

Mother tending sheep (Luxor 1952)

A candid kiddo at nine (Alexandria 1953)

08

Mother in her prime (Madrid 1958)

Father in his fifties (Alexandria 1959)

At sixteen. Too young to be a soldier
(Alexandria 1960)

CHAPTER ELEVEN

My father had nothing to hide, to fear, or to lose when the 1952 Revolution came and a totalitarian, military Regime took over the country. He was only a little frightened of the general unrest and of the long shadow of the *Mokhabarat* whose informers were eavesdropping everywhere.

Except with a very few, close, dear friends, he always felt uncomfortable with people in general and colleagues in particular—with whom he had nothing in common. In the early fifties he suffered a very tragic ordeal: his reputation was endangered and his livelihood might have been ruined.

In 1952, when we were still living in the Victoria district, grave accusations of some kind were brought against him by a Government school-inspector and supervisor, a despicable douche bag named Khalifa Mekki whom my mother called a swine because he was short, fat piggy-faced with small, red, naughty, wild boar eyes. My father's salary was withheld and he wasn't rehabilitated till months later, when a Board of Enquiry found him innocent and cleared him. I wondered what accusations the swine could have brought against him; not for laxity, unpunctuality or laziness and surely not for corruption and embezzlement. School teachers are too unimportant to be touched by such matters, which are far beyond their scope.

I was too young then to realise the extent of our tragedy though I clearly recall two things. First is that our friend Baraka came to the rescue and helped out financially until my father got back his salary and the arrears; and second, and most dramatic to me, is that we had so little money that mother couldn't even buy knickers and wore my old underpants which would have otherwise been thrown away.

Mom had a strong character. She was pushy, authoritarian and fearless. When she married she automatically became an Egyptian citizen but, when things got tough in Egypt and exit visas for Egyptian nationals became difficult to obtain, she rushed to the Spanish Consulate in Alexandria to recover her former nationality. She thus became a foreigner in Egypt and was issued with a resident's card that she regularly renewed.

She didn't fear the dreadful *Mokhabarat* whom she considered a gang of morons compared to the *Checa* (the red militia) she had to face during the Spanish Civil War.

In the early sixties, the situation in Egypt rapidly deteriorated. The shops emptied as there wasn't any hard currency available to import "accessory" goods not indispensable to the country. The Russians were in place and the capital was all invested in building the Aswan dam and replenishing Nasser's arsenals.

Mother wished to get me out of the country presto and back to Spain with my aunt, as soon as I had passed my *baccalauréat* (French high-school diploma).

In 1962, she was appointed a teacher of Spanish at the Spanish Cultural Centre. She made some money (which is what she always wanted) while socialising and having fun in her work. She was prized and cherished by colleagues and scholars and taught the language to many students, amongst them some school friends of mine.

My parents never felt joy or happiness to transmit or to share, yet they had a great sense of duty, responsibility, justice and high moral values. I esteem these virtues above any others, as joy and happiness are more often than not the shelter of fools.

Except for rare, happy moments their world was grey and wrapped in Spanish and Egyptian shades of the past. I cannot tell if their marriage was successful or not, but I know they loved each other in their own distant and special way.

In 1969, my mother returned to Spain for good. Dad, who had retired years before, came once a year to Madrid and stayed with us for several months. Both of them also visited Bilbao and Majorca while I was working there.

After his 1974 visit he stopped coming and then he stopped writing his bi-monthly letters. One day his nephew Fuad sent a telegram saying that he was in hospital. Two days later another cable announced that he had died after a very short agony. He was seventy-four years old. I am sure that he was good and ready when death knocked on his door. Maybe his whole life had only been a training ground for the final departure.

When I visited Alexandria in November 2010, Yorgho told me that a few months before his demise my father summoned him to help destroy and dispose of photographs and old documents he had been accumulating for years. He knew that Yorgho was my best friend, that he was loyal and discreet. "What's the use of all these papers", he told him "They're more than forty years old." He probably felt that he would die soon and wished to erase the memories of his past which would interest no-one.

In a letter I received from Fuad weeks after father passed away, he wrote that one morning, summoned by our faithful maid Chérifa who cleaned and cooked for him, he found out that my father had collapsed the day before and had spent the night unconscious on the bedroom floor until Chérifa arrived early the following morning.

He immediately took him to hospital where he died two days later, apparently from senility. He also wrote that in his final moments the only language he could still speak or understand was Spanish. He had forgotten all the other languages he spoke including Arabic, which was his native tongue.

His long journey was over. He had been weary and dissatisfied for a long time. He had had it and wanted to let go. When one is dead, it's of no importance if one has lived for twenty or for ninety years. When I'm dead, the memory of my father which I am now reviving will be totally and definitively consigned to oblivion.

Our friends the Barakas had a kitchen-garden where the cook *Mabruka* grew vegetables and flowers. Their two storey villa was surrounded by tall buildings and whenever I played and hid amongst the greenery I had the impression of being spied on by peeping neighbours.

The Barakas kept hens for meat and eggs and a couple of presumptuous and wrathful red-crested turkeys which started a pursuit and tried to get me as soon as they saw me minding my p's and q's, or busily and absent-mindedly feeding the hens.

At times, *Mabruka* slaughtered a chicken by first making a tiny incision in the bird's throat with a small knife and then releasing it amongst the others. For a few seconds, the bird, unaware that its life was over, joined the rest of the coop and kept on walking, cackling and pecking. But very soon and very suddenly, a red stream began to gush from the wound and the hen fell to the ground in violent spasms, while being emptied of its blood.

A tragedy hit the Barakas soon after we moved to Victoria. Lula's seventeen-year old brother, who lived with their parents in a neighbouring, large family house called respectfully "the big house" (not a jail), sneaked into his school building one night looking for quick cash—which wasn't there as he had been misinformed and there was no money on the premises.

He was probably noisy in his search or swept his flashlight around once too often, because the caretaker sleeping in the premises woke-up and surprised him while he was searching the drawers in the headmaster's office. The boy panicked, stabbed the man seven times with his pocket knife and ran away. The janitor died that same night after identifying his assailant. When the police caught up with him at home, at three in the morning, he was in the bathroom washing the blood from his hands, clothes and knife.

He was not sentenced to death by hanging because he was under age but received a life sentence with hard labour. Fifteen years later he died in prison of tuberculosis a consequence of harsh treatment and malnourishment.

It was a hard blow for his family, who belonged to the high stratum of Alexandria's middle-class. Friends were also puzzled and wondered what had pushed the young man to commit such a heinous murder. We later discovered that his father was a penny-pincher who hardly provided him with any pocket-money, and that the boy had been lately misguided and driven to larceny by a gang of older punks and thieves. He had killed the caretaker out of childish fear. The man had recognized him as a school student and if he had talked he surely have had to face severe punishment and expulsion.

Lula, his sister and the only person of the family we knew was devastated. My mother tried to comfort her as best as she could. She admitted that her brother, although very young, unconscious and irresponsible, was an assassin and had wrecked the lives of two families. The victim had a wife and four children, who were left unprotected as no indemnities or any kind of help were considered at the time. After the trial was over and sentence passed, his name was never again mentioned in her home.

In November 2010, Yorgho and I visited my old district of Victoria after forty-six years of absence.

The Farida's house and garden were gone and replaced by a large condo building. I stood there on the corner of her street and remembered those warm, balmy summer nights filled with the dizzying smell of jasmine when I used to walk my dog around the block. I often crossed her doorstep and lingered there to hear her teasing little voice calling from the bedroom to her German grandfather "Opa (grandfather) . . . .

"Opa, Opa" . . . .

The four-storey edifice where we had lived for three years was still there, well—preserved except for a dirty façade. Most of the surrounding villas including the Calza palace had been demolished and supplanted by large buildings. The narrow streets were unpaved and dusty and jammed with dirty cars parked everywhere, which made the streets look even tighter. The *caracol* opposite our apartment, where suspects were interrogated and tortured was now a primary school.

The Barakas villa was still there, almost untouched by time. I rang the bell and a man in his fifties came to a first floor window. He was surprised to see someone he didn't know talk to him about his family in English and Arabic.

I told him who I was, the son of Mr Wahby, Baraka's best friend. He came downstairs and invited us in. He wore a *galabiya* which is also used as a man's nightgown. It's loose and comfortable and through bottomless pockets (if one wishes), one can scratch one's balls thoroughly and inconspicuously.

Still standing on the doorstep, he told me that Baraka and his wife Lula were dead (which I knew) and that they died childless (which I also knew); he was Lula's nephew and had inherited the property.

I was tempted to bring up the subject of his uncle (Lula's brother), the boy killer who one night, almost sixty years ago, dispatched the school caretaker and died in prison. But I didn't mention that drama. Better not.

When the tragedy hit his family, this man was not yet born and probably was never told the story to preserve the family honour and good name. He looked like a kind and peaceful man and I had no right to give him distress.

He again invited us to join him for tea and cakes. I was about to accept his invitation as I wanted to take pictures of the house and the kitchen-garden I felt was my own and where I played for so many hours. But Yorgho, standing at a distance discouraged me. I shouldn't have listened to him. We just thanked the man for his time and drove out of Victoria.

On 23rd July, 1952 in Cairo and 26th July, in Alexandria (a few months after the orchestrated burning by a mob of more than two-hundred of Cairo's "symbols of British imperialism"), the "free officers" (a military junta) removed King Farouk from the throne of Egypt and brought in the Republic. We hardly felt or knew at the time of the real consequences of this event that brought down one hundred and fifty years of a single, uninterrupted dynasty and dramatically changed the lives of hundreds of thousands of people forever.

Shortly after the revolution most Egyptians and *khawagat* felt happy for the country as they believed that this uprising, apart from bringing down a rotten, shameful, and outdated Monarchy, would end with Egypt's corruption. It would also enhance social justice and bring solace to the poor with the implementation of overdue and must—needed land reforms by taking some property (but not all) from the extremely rich Pashas who owned most of the Egyptian agricultural land and farms.

A couple of days before the "coup" my mother had what she thought was a premonitory dream involving general disorder, anarchy and violence ending with the death of the King. As it turned out, King Farouk was not murdered but deposed and expelled. He and his family were granted first-class tickets to a golden exile in Italy on the Royal Yacht *Mahrussa*.

The King and his Court sailed away from Alexandria where he was spending his summer holiday alternating between his two palaces of *Montazah* and *Ras el Tin*. He left without hindrance, his vast luggage unchecked and filled with many goodies of a golden nature. His journey took him first to the isle of Capri then to (before its time) the dolce vita in Rome.

He was soon forgotten, except by the gossip magazines, and died in 1965 when he suddenly collapsed in a Roman restaurant. The Egyptian secret-services came under scrutiny as they were suspected of poisoning his lobster but nothing could be proved.

The bottom line of the story is that one fine summer day almighty Farouk left his Cairo palace for his yearly vacation in Alexandria and was never to see his country again.

At the outbreak of the Revolution, there was discussion among the "free officers" about what should be done with the King. Some of them thought that he was a traitor—amongst other things because of his involvement in the acquisition of faulty arms for the 1948 war—should be sentenced to death and executed. Nevertheless Colonel Nasser chose to look lenient in the eyes of the world and those Arab Monarchies who didn't trust him and were watching very closely. Egypt played a dominant role in the Arab League and a man like Nasser could be of great danger to the decadent kingdoms spread throughout the Middle East and the Gulf.

He thus convinced his cronies to spare the King's life and to let him sail into the sunset. As Nasser stated later, his Revolution had been bloodless from the start and he didn't want it bloodied by the death of one individual, no matter how much the King deserved to die.

The fatherly figure of General Naguib, who became the first Egyptian President in 1952, represented the white Revolution's façade behind which the famished wolves hid, with Colonel Nasser as the leader of the pack and cronies amongst whom were the future President Sadat, and hashish-smoker Amer who would become Field Marshall. Other officers of different ranks completed the Revolutionary gallery.

General Naguib was soon deposed and rewarded for his loyal services with permanent house-arrest which lasted until he died, many years later.

My mother's dream was not a premonition. Dreams are not crystal balls and they do not disclose the secrets of the future as the future only exists when it becomes the present. She was probably worried by the anxiety lingering in the air on the days preceding the Revolution. Dreams are only the reflection of hopeless expectations, buried frustrations and all the wants, hates and fears concealed in one's mind.

Nasser must have later regretted his decision to spare the King, when he discovered that Farouk, a teetotaller, had smuggled out of the country in the yacht that took him away a fortune in gold ingots hidden in empty crates of whisky he claimed were for his personal consumption. He must have also resented that the ex-King was still considered one of the richest men in the world, the huge fortune he had plundered from Egypt stashed away in Swiss bank accounts. His endless excesses, well publicised in the media, were shaming the new image of Nasser's post-revolutionary Egypt.

His degrading downfall had obviously taught Farouk nothing and instead of seeking oblivion and forgiveness he was behaving as the selfish swine he always was to the eyes of the world.

Handsome Gamal (Nasser's name) was probably filled with rage, impotence and frustration towards the fat, clownish ex-King who was teasing him with his usual display of debauchery.

Nasser could have deplored this situation with his cronies just as King Henry the Second of England did centuries before him when he pricked his Barons to murder Thomas Becket. The Egyptian Barons eager to please their *Raïs* might have commandeered a death squad which, in spite of its vicious mission, was quick and merciful in getting to the ex-King's stomach, the seat of his most treasured pleasure, by slipping a painless poison into his food. His mistress, who was also at the table and who could have been involved in the assassination, disappeared soon after never to be found. Farouk could also have died of a stroke or a heart attack, as his corpulence and lifestyle vouched for it. The real cause of his death is not relevant; he died without knowing what hit him with a bellyful of delicacies and a beautiful woman by his side. 'Tis a consummation devoutly to be wished".

A comic scene from a movie describing his dilapidated life could be the grand finale in the Roman restaurant when he crumples up, sinking his head into the remains of his lobster and collapses on the floor, his face painted with a mixture of different sauces. It could be the perfect ending for the unbelievable extravaganza his public and private image symbolised during his short and useless (except for him) life.

What seems preposterous and makes this kill-the-king plan hard to believe is that President Nasser waited thirteen years to carry it out.

In 1965, ex-King Farouk was no longer a threat to anyone as Egypt was beyond the pale. The lands and fortunes had been confiscated a long time ago. What remained of European Management and know-how had almost vanished and what was left would soon be erased after the 1967 six-day war. The country had a Russian flavour and Nasser had long lost his credibility. Like an unconscious or unlucky gambler, he had been playing the wrong cards, bluffing his way around and making the wrong decisions on national and international issues. His nemesis was just two years away, when the Egyptian armies were wiped out during the June 1967 six-day war with Israel. He survived for three more years and died in 1970.

Therefore, if the plot to murder the ex-King was genuine, I think it should be perceived within the frame of Nasser's frustrations, resentfulness, envy and craving for revenge, which focused on the ex-Monarch and what he stood for. These considerations must have weighed on him and played a decisive part in Farouk's possible murder more than any other political or financial consideration.

CHAPTER TWELVE

In 1953, we moved from Victoria to the district of Camp-César. We rented an apartment on the sixth floor of a ten-storey brand-new building with a lift exceptional in those days as not many were tall enough to have one. School was only three hundred metres away and from the towering height of her balcony Mom could see me come and go and watch the company I kept while I played in the garden below.

There were two brothers at school named Jean and Jacques. The former was my classmate and a testosterone-free potential faggot. If you touched or even brushed him lightly, he would giggle and fidget like little girls do, while wriggling his big fat arse. At the movies, he loved extinguishing his cigarettes on the back of the seat in front and watching the glowing embers cascading onto the carpet like lava spurting out of a volcano. Smoking was allowed inside cinemas and the air was thick with fumes and stale with stench; movie fans were therefore passive smokers but, then, as we were ignorant and unconscious of the grave dangers of tobacco we luckily suffered no harm and grew-up strong and healthy.

The father of the two boys, a wealthy businessman, owned the one and only V8 convertible, yellow Cadillac Eldorado in Alexandria—if not in Egypt. Everyday he drove his car to school to pick up his sons, who climbed into the back, looking like the heirs to the lost crown while we watched in awe as they slowly drove away. King Farouk owned many Cadillacs and dozens of other upmarket cars and, for reasons probably involving immediate recognition, all his vehicles were red; by Royal decree he was the only person in Egypt allowed to own red automobiles.

On Saturday evenings, we used to go to a double-feature programme, either to the Odeon, (now closed after being for some time a Chinese shopping arcade) or to the Gaité (now a new shopping-centre) both walking distance from home. We could not always afford the luxurious cinemas downtown like the Metro, exclusively showing MGM pictures or the 20th Century Fox cinema Amir. Other movie-houses such as the Rialto, Royal or Strand showed the productions from other major Hollywood Studios.

The ticket for the first-class theatres for one movie, a cartoon and an American newsreel was double what we paid in our neighbourhood cinemas for two of those same films shown there five or six months later. By being a little patient, we got two pictures for the price of one. The catch was that when they reached the "second-hand circuit" they were aggressively cut to fit into three daily sessions of three hours each—a common practice in those cinemas.

I was a film fan but my father thought that there wasn't much to learn from them.

All through the years I "swallowed" a lot of Hollywood crap. I didn't care much about the quality as all I wanted was to be entertained by the most popular, *macho* stars in the business, by real *hombres* like Paul Newman, Kirk Douglas, John Wayne, Rock Hudson (ooops sorry) and others whom I tried to imitate by copying their gestures and demeanour. The "dream factory" stopped when the last image had vanished from the screen, the curtain had been drawn and I was on the street again facing the ugly realities of the daily life I had managed to forget for a few magic hours.

European art movies seldom came our way and when they did, we weren't ready for them. The three hour's long Visconti masterpiece *Il Gattopardo*, (the Leopard) was considered "slow and boring". The first day it was exhibited in its full uncut version, but when it was shown the following day, it had been savagely mutilated to fit into the under two-hour, commercial mark.

Dad called Westerns *los dos caballos atados* (the two tied-up horses) and he was right because if you carefully watch a Western, two or three horses are "parked" most of the time outside saloons or the Sheriff's office.

I booked our tickets on Fridays and always tried to get the same numbered seats for Saturday's second show starting at six thirty. The fat Greek woman cashier at the Odeon box office crossed out with a blue marker the seats I pointed-out to her on the plan displaying the stalls and wrote down the numbers on the tickets. I paid seven piaster (one cent of a euro) per ticket and left a small baksheesh (tip). I still remember our usual seats: aisle, numbers 116, 118 and 120; even numbers were located on the right an odd numbers on the left.

In Egypt, women are appraised by most men not only for their virtues as good wives and housekeepers but also for their body weight. Egyptians love their women with thick thighs, big bosoms and large arses and fondly call them *batta* (ducky) because of the sexy way they walk, swaying their plump bodies like juicy ducks. Slim women are undervalued and could remain single as a would-be husband might feel cheated if he married a suspiciously anorexic character, so fashionable in our society nowadays.

Just like women, movies in Egypt were also appreciated for their weight. Before the film started there was censorship notice in which the weight of the picture was briefly displayed on the screen. Each kilo of a thirty-five millimetres film is equivalent to five minutes' screening. If the film weighed eighteen kilos (i.e. ninety minutes) it was fair and square the average length of an American film in those days. If the film weighed more than twenty kilos the crowd got ecstatic and applauded joyfully. But if the film was under ninety minutes, the public roared and kicked the seats and whistled in discontent till the main titles appeared when they would calm down. What they generally didn't know or cared about was that pictures were regularly cut to fit the neighbourhood cinemas' tight schedule.

The audience yelled and cheered during action scenes in support of the good guys. They also whistled and sighed loudly when the actors romanced and kissed. I liked the candid, spontaneous humour of those displays as much as I enjoyed the film itself; it was like watching a live show with a roaring audience.

My father didn't appreciate those spells he called the "uncivilised display of bad manners". He disapprovingly looked around him, shook his head in bewilderment and wondered what manner of human cattle was sharing his vital space.

On Monday mornings, the narrow, dusty Odeon back alley was covered with cuts of celluloid leftovers, thrown by the projectionist from his cabin-window, probably to please moviegoers like me, who rushed there almost at dawn to pick them up. Back home we used a magnifying glass to enlarge the thirty five millimetres frames and see the actors and scenes from films we had viewed the previous week.

The films, mostly American, where shown in English with subtitles in French and Arabic, allowing everyone to follow the storyline either by listening or reading. If during the projection the Arabic subtitles inadvertently remained hidden below the image level, the audience would shout at the top of their voices *targama, targama* (translation, translation)

My Italian neighbour Bruno was an only child. His one-armed father, over six feet tall, slightly under one hundred and forty kilos was a hell of a dictator, who spread fear and insecurity in his household.

He probably spent World War Two in a concentration camp—when Italy joined Germany in World War Two—as the British rounded up all Italians and put them away for the duration of the conflict.

To make up for the loss of his arm and instead of strengthening his other limb as cripples often do, he developed instead an astonishing and incredible spitting power. He could spit farther and stronger than anyone else. The devastating spittle freshly fired from his infamous mouth could burn like a spoonful of molten metal when, from a distance of up to five metres, it reached the back of his victim's neck (his favourite target). He often practised this unique skill on his son, especially when the boy had misbehaved and was trying to escape from his father's wrath. In a split second, when Bruno thought he was safely out of reach, the blazing liquid would hit its target . . . . Gotcha!! one could almost hear the dirty swine say.

They lived on the ground floor of the building bordering the public garden we all shared. That fat man was also a peeping Tom and his favourite observation post was behind his half-closed window-shutters from where he inconspicuously kept a watchful eye on the comings and goings of the neighbourhood.

In spite of having a foul father, Bruno was a nice boy, very patriotic in the best Italian pre-war tradition. He attended the Italian *Istituto Don Bosco* and was sincerely convinced that the flag of his country was the most beautiful flag in the world. He said that his beloved colours of green, red and white were wholesome and lovelier than the blue, white and red of the French flag or the red and gold of the Spanish one.

When I asked for a logical explanation he replied without doubt or hesitation that "once upon a time" all the flags of the world were assembled "somewhere" and that an artless half-witted child was asked to kiss the one he loved best amongst all he colours on display. Without hesitation, the tot immediately identified and kissed the Italian banner and that was that. He never told me the origin of that senseless story but I suspected that it was his rogue and authoritarian father who probably took him for a moron.

Homosexuality and paedophilia are taboo topics in Egypt, rarely discussed disclosed or acknowledged. The sense of values and sex practices of the population within the different layers of society vary according to contrasting moral issues. If a man has sex with a boy or with another man he is not considered *khawal* (homosexual) as long as he acts like a man i.e. being the giver and not the taker. The faggot is always the one on the receiving end playing the woman's role. For alien mentalities the concept is difficult to understand and though not totally correct, bisexual is the closest word for it.

Two notorious paedophiles both in their mid-forties lived in my neighbourhood. One of them was Nino. He was Italian and lived with his sister at the end of my street in a wooden house with a garden. He was a small-time electrician who displayed a screwdriver behind one ear as trademark of his craft and a scrounged filter cigarette on the other. He was handy and we relied on him for minor jobs around the house such as changing fuses and switches or repairing short circuits. Though we knew him for what he was, he kept coming to us for a bit of conversation. He spoke French and as a neighbour we considered him more like a friend than a foe.

His "honey-pot-trick" as we called it was to tell us lads that he had in one of his trouser pockets some loose change or a couple of those large and tempting marbles we used in our games. "All you have to do is go for it", he said maliciously. If one complied, the innocent hand would discover soon enough that the recompense was none other than a couple of larger than life hairy *cojones* (balls) hidden at the bottom of his torn pocket, bigger by any standards than the expected multicoloured marbles. On top of the *cojones* there was also a stiff club for which we had no use as we didn't practise golf.

We were accustomed to his stratagem and we never took the bait (some kids did) although he kept tirelessly repeating his number just for the fun of it. All in all he was a nice man, never out of line.

However, my suspicious mother, aware of his little schemes and thinking that I was naïve and awkward (true) and in very great danger of losing my innocence (false) in such a revolting way, summoned him to ask what his intentions were. He promised that my friends and I would never be the victims of his depraved lust for little boys. Reassured, my mother and he became friends. Those were the days when unsavoury matters were settled amicably—as long as I was out of harm's way. Years later Nino and his sister sold their house and moved to Italy. The buyers, a real estate and construction company demolished it and built in its place a fifteen-story condo.

The other *Betaa el ayal* (pederast; the correct translation is "one who likes children") sharing the market with Nino was Amin. He was a fat, sweaty Lebanese with yellowish, crooked teeth, who kept a bookstore not far from the Odeon cinema. I visited him once a week to buy school stationary and two French magazines: *Tintin* and the *Journal de Mickey*. I always found him seated behind his counter, constantly filling, lighting and smoking a pipe whose sweet aroma filled the room. He brushed my fingers when he took my money and proposed a visit to the back shop where he kept, he said, many fine books and magazines I had never seen before and would very much enjoy. I smiled but as soon as I got my change, I waved and ran away. I pictured Amin as a big, hairy spider standing on the edge of its web waiting for juicy little kiddos to drop in.

Those were harmless East Mediterranean pederasts only longing for conversation and a few caresses. They didn't abduct rape or kill children, and the infamous paedophilia business now carried out on the net was not yet mediatised and blown out of proportion. In present circumstances, considering how sensitive the paedophilia situation has become, any one of the minor incidents related above would have been reported to the police, resulting in hearings and trials that would cause unnecessary shame and pain to all parties concerned.

Egyptian cuisine was off-limits at home except for some special delicacies we all enjoyed such as "stuffed vine-leaves" and Greek *mussaka* cooked Egyptian style, heavy on chopped meat, baked potato slices and egg-plant.

Mother favoured Spanish cuisine above any other. On Saturdays or Sundays she cooked paella, considered by one-time tourists ignorant about Spain as the most typical Spanish dish. Paella is made of rice to which other varied ingredients are added such as pieces of meat, red peppers, saffron, shellfish and chicken. In Arabic the word paella is *bakeya* (leftovers), because in Arab Spain, to avoid wasting food, the leftovers from the day before were added to the following day's rice.

Mom only cooked with olive oil. She loathed Egyptian products such as *samna* (fat) or other vegetable oil. She bought the drums from the Spanish ships which docked twice a month in Alexandria. She had befriended the Captains and Officers through the staff of the Spanish Consulate and, at times, she gained access to the docks where the ship's crew delivered to her a ten-litre drum. "It's a little expensive but worth it," she used to say.

The Egyptian food I loved most was also the cheapest. It was the popular *fool* (cooked brown beans) and falafel which feed the entire Egyptian population.

My father enjoyed telling a silly joke, a *jeu de mots* (pun) only understandable by those who know English and French. It says that when the English wanted to denigrate the Egyptians (which they often did) they called them names like "bloody fools". The Egyptians, however, misunderstood the insult and gently smiled believing the khawaga meant a *plat de fool* (a plate of beans). It's a very foolish joke but so at times was my father's sense of humour.

Falafel is made of fava beans soaked overnight, shaped into small balls, and fried in boiling oil. A full meal in one of those popular restaurants was called *fool* and falafel and included boiled eggs, pita (Arab bread), *homos* and a tomato. It was cheaper, tastier and healthier than any fast food. The nearest *fool* and falafel restaurant was located on the street corner opposite the Odeon cinema. Yorgho and I often stopped there for a quick bite and a Coke. The cook who chopped the beans was a Copt named Aisa. He was short-sighted and wore spectacles with lenses as thick as bottle bottoms.

One day in the middle of summer when we walked into the restaurant, Aisa was busy preparing his falafel dough, vigorously turning the handle of the grinder triturating the beans into a pulp. He was so close to the oil cauldron that he was perspiring, the sweat from his forehead dripping onto his glasses. So absorbed in his work, he didn't see through the misted lenses that a large flying *sorsar* (cockroach) had dropped through the jaws of the machine into the bean mix. When he had finished, he rolled the dough into balls, fried them and served us, at no extra cost, a hot plate of protein-enriched falafel.

At the start of the school term, on 29th October, 1956, the British, French and Israeli forces launched a tripartite offensive to repossess the "jewel of Egypt", the Suez Canal which had been nationalised by Nasser. American and Russian diplomatic pressure prevented a full invasion of the country, forcing the aggressors to withdraw a few days later. It was an illogical and stupid action carried out by "sensible" powers which achieved nothing except destroy their already troubled relations with the Egyptian regime and jeopardise the lives of Egypt's foreign community. The fact is they were not comfortable with the dubious and fickle path the country was taking under the dictatorship in place since the 1952 revolution.

Each of the would-be invaders greedily longed for a piece of the Egyptian cake: Britain was inconsolable (as Britain always is when kicked out of somewhere) for losing the Suez Canal and its lucrative income; France wished to topple President Nasser and put an end to his dreadful influence and support to Algeria, still a French colony fighting for its independence; Israel, looking to protect and reinforce its 1948 borders, joined the big boys hoping that in the ensuing *mêlée*, it could inconspicuously expand its territory by adding as much Egyptian soil as possible.

The town of Port Said was heavily bombed and marked out for the landing of the first "allied" troops, who would then proceed to Cairo, get rid of Nasser, bring down the government, name one of their choosing and return to the good old times of colonisation. I wonder how Britain and France could have even thought of such an irresponsible line of action, especially in the second half of the twentieth century when imperialism was on the decline and third-world countries had gained or were on the way to recovering their independence. Maybe it was a last stand to avoid the inevitable loss of their colonies.

For the duration of the war, schools were shut and Egyptian teachers were mobilized to participate in civil defence. They were provided with uniforms and *Maüser* rifles dating back to the Second World War but which were still in use as standard equipment in the Egyptian Armed Forces. These improvised recruits had no military training and were given no ammunition to prevent them from hurting each other or inadvertently injuring or killing other people.

Their mission was to watch the skies for the expected waves of enemy paratroopers, with orders to take them prisoners as soon as they landed. If the *franga* (a distortion of the word French meaning foreigner; its origin dates back to the time of the crusades in the Levant) resisted arrest, they were allowed to give them the bayonet or, if overwhelmed by their numbers and fire power, they could ask for help from the ever-present crowd to give them a severe beating, first with sticks, then with stones if the enemy tried to run away (throwing stones is a popular pastime and children are very good shots).

In any case, the *franga* would not have been beaten or stoned, but cut to pieces and not by the men from the civil defence, but by the angry rabble, whose hate for the enemy and all foreigners was constantly fuelled during the war days on radio and newspapers. It was amusing and pathetic to watch those guys (amongst them my geography teacher) walking all day long, up and down the streets, their noses in the air searching for white specks in the sky.

Fortunately, action took place only around the town of Port Said and Suez Canal area and no British or French paratrooper ever landed in Alexandria to enjoy its autumn charms.

When air raids were announced at night and sirens started to whine everyone yelled as loudly as possible, "*Taffi el nur*" (switch off the lights) which became as popular and repetitive as a hit song: bawled by husky black *bawab*, patriotic passers-by and neighbours with the privilege of having powerful, resounding voices. They were orchestrated by the men from the civil defence, who hollered louder than the rest. The headlights of all vehicles were painted blue and we covered our window-panes with mauve cellophane paper.

One evening at the movies, Dad surprised us with a show of courage and phlegm. It was still daylight and the picture was well on its way when the sirens started. The doors were opened for immediate evacuation and the audience panicked and rushed out like cattle on a stampede. My father didn't budge from his seat and told us to stay put and remain calm; "No need to get trampled by the frightened multitude," he said. "No bomb is going to hit this place anyway." When the crowd had left, we leisurely abandoned the premises and walked back home. I thought it very cool of him.

No bombs were dropped that day or on any other day and, like many others, the alert was a false alarm. Alexandria was not a strategic position; fortunately we were spared the conflict and left in peace.

The 1956 October war marked the beginning of the end for Egypt's European Community. As a direct consequence of the offensive, French and British citizens (including our teachers) were immediately arrested and expelled from the country. Foreign schools were re-organized and a new teaching staff was hired. Greek, Armenian and Egyptian teachers took over the vacant posts left by our "departed French" and the Lycée re-opened its doors at the end of November. One year later, following a change of mood of the Egyptian government, our French teachers were allowed to return. But in 1961, at the height of the Algerian-French conflict they were again expelled—this time for good—, in another of Nasser's nationalistic flings when he was supporting the Algerians with money and weapons in their fight for independence.

All through the post-revolution years links between Egypt and the west were tense and suspicious. It was not till the early seventies when Nasser was finally dead and the Russians had left that his successor President Sadat normalized Egypt's international relations and signed a peace agreement with Israel, a circumstance which led to his assassination in 1981.

Our Lycée was renamed *Al Horreya* (liberty) and things changed. The teaching of Arabic became a priority not only for Egyptians but for foreigners too. The new staff was efficient and tried to keep up with the teaching standards of their French predecessors. In spite of the recent events, our Egyptian schoolmasters still respected their French counterparts, humiliated and expelled from the country. The following anecdote substantiates this point:

In 1960, when the French were back, two of my classmates—both named Mahmud—sat side by side on a front bench. One was tall and good looking, a bit of a bully and a strong supporter of Nasser; I didn't trust him as I feared he might be a snitcher. He later became an army officer, fought the 1967 six days' war, left the military and became an actor. The other Mahmud was short, with dark skin, green eyes and a polio leg. Quiet and unobtrusive, he thrived as an engineer in the oil business, worked in the deserts of Libya and Algeria, took early retirement and moved to Canada where he now lives.

Mr Vié our French literature teacher always mispronounced their name, making it sound like "mammoth" every time he called either of them, making us laugh foolishly time and again. During his classes, Mr Vié often didn't use the table but grabbed his chair and sat amongst us. He took off his shoes (he always wore the same unpolished brown sandals and dark green socks though he wasn't Irish) and placed both feet on the edge of the bench where the two Mahmud sat, his feet facing their faces; he then tipped his chair, keeping his balance on its two legs and started his lesson. He was a short man with small feet that surely didn't reek but neither smelled like roses. Such behaviour was a lack of respect towards his students, especially in a country where feet and shoes are not considered very noble attributes.

The two boys bravely took their grievance to our Arabic language teacher, Mr Wafa, a member of the school board, whose seniority and authority went beyond that of any other teacher. He listened sympathetically, tapping the tip of his pencil on his desk as he always did when he felt nervous or annoyed and gently replied that he was really sorry but that there was nothing he could do, considering that Mr Vié was a French teacher with certain privileges and thus couldn't be troubled with such trivial matters concerning his lack of civility.

In his early twenties Mr Vié was fresh from University and an excellent teacher in spite of his limited experience. In random conversations we had about cars and other topics, he told us that he had had a driving license since he was eighteen but that cars terrified him and he never drove one in France or Alexandria. Many years later I was told that he died in a car crash while driving in the South of France. Was it a premonition, a lack of experience or kismet? Let the wheel of fortune turn.

CHAPTER THIRTEEN

After the October 1956 war, my mother was determined to leave Egypt. She knew that from then on, things would go from bad to worse and she was damn right. The failed tripartite offensive provided President Nasser and his government with the golden opportunity they needed to start the appropriation of Jewish and foreign properties. He launched a wild, discriminatory campaign and nationalised (official word for steal) foreign capital and other assets forcing non-Egyptians to leave the country (many of them penniless) and look for a living elsewhere. The Jews, who had been for ages an important tool in the Egyptian economy, were first targeted because of Egypt's antagonism to the State of Israel.

Our next-door neighbours, a family of five left for the United States early in 1957 and took along as their only asset two fifty-kilo sacks of onions (probably imported from Spain) that they expected to sell in America as the foothold for a new business.

Furthermore, since the 1952 July Revolution, the Egyptian Pashas who possessed the land and the wealth and who had ruled Egypt for centuries were on the final leg to reconversion. Their lands had been confiscated, cut down to *fedan* (acres) and redistributed to the *fellaheen*. This policy proved unproductive as the peasants grew weary of cultivating such small areas of soil that could hardly support their families.

Today, almost sixty years have passed and nothing has changed in Egypt. The old Pashas are long gone although the titles of Pasha and *Bey* are not forgotten by the people and are still used by the man in the street to address those individuals whom they deem to respect for their wealth or background; they still cannot forget the "good old days" although three generations have elapsed. Millions of Egyptians have fled the country and are living and working all over the world. Should they return one day en masse to the motherland (most improbable) in search of jobs, the economic chaos would be indescribable.

Today's "new" Egyptian Pashas are the *nouveaux riches*, a minority elite formed by entrepreneurs, tradesmen, professionals, hashish smugglers and rotten politicians, who make and steal and spend money as if there were no tomorrow. In the midst of a large, impoverished population, their excesses range from lavish gardened houses in Cairo to summer resort villas, luxurious cars, wedding banquets for thousands in the best hotels and impressive accounts in foreign banks.

As for the fellaheen and the poor who escape from impoverished rural areas to look for jobs in large cities, things have changed for the worse. They are hit there by a severe housing crisis, massive unemployment, squalid living conditions and the main cause of all evils: overpopulation caused by an unstoppable increase in the birth-rate which adds more than two million every year to the inhabitants of Egypt.

I am fully convinced that this nightmarish overpopulation problem, which is getting worse day by day, will finally bring the country to its knees . . . . and what next? Will the Muslim brotherhood (fundamentalists) who are now so generous in helping the poor with funds they receive from Saudi Arabia, take over the country (with the help of the army), send the wealthy classes to oblivion and start distributing *misery per tutti* (misery for all) except for themselves?

Over-crowding in developing countries (unstoppable whatever some may think) and ever-shrinking world resources will in the future spread misfortune *ad infinitum* and will negatively affect rich and easygoing societies here and there, which had thrived on the misery of others.

It won't be nice to live during the second half of the twenty-first century and for those who do, it might be a dreadful experience; life could become a nightmare to which man will of course adapt to as he has always done following evolutionary tendencies.

The exodus of foreigners, which started after the 1952 Revolution, continued until 5th June, 1967 six-day war which finished off those unwanted Jews who were still sticking around, refusing to leave Egypt.

Like German Jews in the thirties, they refused to believe that they could be dispossessed, harmed and expelled from a country which they considered their own. In spite of the premonitory events of the last fifteen years, they were still refusing to accept the reality of the evolving situation, and kept clinging to their dreams in a country they had lost.

On the morning of 5th June, 1967, on the same day the six-day war started, one male Jew from each Jewish family was arrested, taken directly to a local Police Station and then dispatched by special train to the infamous prison of Abu Zaabal not far from Cairo but in the middle of nowhere. Those men never saw their homes again. Months after the war was over, they were progressively released from captivity and taken under military surveillance to Cairo airport, for immediate deportation. Their families, who would later rejoin them, met them at the airport to give them money, a suitcase with their personal belongings and a "bon voyage" goodbye kiss.

Unfortunately, those first released from prison didn't keep their traps shut and hurried as soon as they arrived in Europe, without a thought for their companions who were still incarcerated, to the BBC and other television and radio channels to tell the world of the unjust and rough treatment they had endured during their captivity in *Abu Zaabal.*

The Egyptian authorities consequently took revenge on those still held in prison making their lives even worse than before. Finally in December the remaining prisoners were released and expelled from Egypt. Those incarcerations were a cruel and meaningless gesture but it achieved what the Regime was after and couldn't achieve before: to drive the very last of the Jewish population out of the country forever.

On that fateful morning of 5th June, 1967, my ex-classmate Robert was playing chess at the home of our friend and also ex-classmate, Tarek. When the police arrived at his address, they were informed by his parents of his whereabouts. They then moved on to Tarek's apartment and took Robert away. The irony of this incident is that, on a morning like any other, Robert (who was born in Egypt and knew no other country) left home to play a game of chess with his friend and never saw Alexandria again until he returned as a visitor, twenty five-years later.

A daunting incident with gloomy, psychological after-effects happened to him the following day when the special convoy from Alexandria carrying Jewish detainees (amongst them Robert) entered Cairo railway station en-route to the prison of *Abu Zaabal.* A huge, mad crowd armed with heavy sticks and shot-guns had taken the platforms by storm, waiting for the train to arrive. The rumour had spread amongst them that the train coming from Alexandria was filled with dangerous Israeli *gasus* (spies) and they were thus determined to beat them to a pulp. Spy is a word not to be used in Egypt; because of the large foreign and Jewish communities, Egyptians were obsessed with spies. In times of crisis they suspected every foreigner or every Jew to be one and even thought that flies were spying on them.

When the train stopped at Cairo Central Station, the fifty or so policemen escorting hundreds of prisoners had a hell of a time to keep them out of harm's way, out of the reach of the demented mob.

These policemen knew that those young men they had brought from Alexandria were not Jewish spies but Egyptian citizens, born and bred there. A young agent candidly asked Robert if he was an Israeli spy to which Robert answered that he was as Egyptian as he. But for the time being, these Jewish were "enemy prisoners" and their responsibility was to deliver them unharmed. They discharged their duty and, disregarding their own safety, provided the necessary protection to get them out of the railway-station and into the waiting buses which took them to the "safety" of the prison.

Robert was profoundly affected by this confrontation and thought it was the end. To this day he hasn't forgotten this ordeal and still cannot stand the sight or the uproar of crowds, whether it's a street demonstration or a bunch of football supporters cheering their team.

The prisoners lived in barracks and slept on the bare floor in groups of seventy, feet to feet. They were given only one blanket which they could use as a mattress, pillow or cover when the weather cooled during winter months. At night they heard strange sounds coming from the kitchen. When they asked the guards, they were told that knives were being sharpened and soon they would all be killed, their throats slit. It was just a joke and the frightful noises were produced by cooks slicing next day's salad with large kitchen knives.

They shared the premises of Abu Zaabal with the persecuted Muslim brotherhood who had been imprisoned there for ages. The Jews and Muslims got along fine. Amongst the latter, there were dentists, general practitioners and barbers and for a small fee one could have a haircut or a tooth cavity filled.

Robert was mostly affected by the lack of solidarity, generosity and compassion he discovered amongst his fellow Jews. The prison food was spartan and those who received money orders could buy extras (whenever available) at the canteen such as cans of meat, fresh fruit, chocolate and cigarettes to complement their diet and needs. The privileged—those who regularly received funds from home—refused to help the needy, who received no assistance from their families. It was shocking and incomprehensible considering they were all in the same shit-hole, subject to the same tyranny, not knowing what the future held in store. It's astounding that such mean behaviour can prevail in such extremes circumstances.

Someone said: "The more I know Man, the less I believe in God." But I prefer a softer, illuminating approach: "The more I distance myself from Man, the closer I get to creation."

Robert was finally released in December 1967 after being held for six months. He was taken to Cairo airport and sent to France. He was stateless and detained at Paris airport. With the help of the French Jewish Community and the Spanish Consulate in Alexandria, he was granted a two-year Spanish passport. A few months later his parents were able to join him in Paris and later they all became French citizens.

According to my latest information there are two Jews left in Alexandria. They are employed by the International Jewish Community to look after the Synagogue and the Jewish cemetery. Both make good money as President and vice-President, but they frequently quarrel because the latter covets the former's title which bears a slightly higher salary. *C'est la vie.*

The years that followed the 1952 military revolution slowly wrecked Egypt's economy. This situation gradually worsened, reaching a climax after the October 1956 Suez war. At that point my mother felt that we would no longer be safe in a country that revived her sad memories of Communist incidents in former Republican Spain. Moreover, after the departure of our French teachers, she was convinced that the Regime would take over all foreign schools and the Lycée Français would become just one more Arab school, which it didn't. Well, not quite.

As a result of this re-structuring we ended up with a mixed French-Egyptian education. Certain subjects were taught in French and others in Arabic. The teaching of Arabic was reinforced and became not only compulsory for all, but indispensable to pass our final examinations. The final high school diploma I passed in 1963 was the *Sanaweya ama*, the Egyptian version of the French *Baccalauréat*. In Spain I validated that title for the Spanish *Bachillerato*.

President Nasser was blindly unaware of his limitations and those of his people. He had the impossible dream of changing his country for the best by reducing poverty and putting an end to the injustice and corruption that had crippled Egypt for centuries. He planned to redistribute wealth in a more equable way and reduce or at least stabilize the increasing birth rate which in the fifties—and as a dark premonition of what is happening today—was already running wild and out of control, though the population was then too small (less than twenty-five millions compared to eighty-five to-day) to make the danger imminent.

Muslims repel communism as it represents the negation of two of the things they most believe in: God and earthly riches which God fervently commands them to pursue.

The United States misunderstood Nasser and came to believe he was a communist, refusing to help when it was most needed; So, feeling rejected, he started to love the more "open-minded" Russians, who built for him the Aswan high dam (Lake Nasser). The Soviets were later rewarded for their assistance and kind cooperation with a kick in the arse, which quickly sent them back to Moscow.

When the Lycée reopened in late November 1956, my mind was elsewhere as I knew that the following summer we would be leaving for Spain. French teachers were already gone and there were new faces around. We had Greek and Armenians teachers for mathematics, science and English and Egyptians for history, geography and other subjects.

CHAPTER FOURTEEN

Classes ended in June 1957 and, on the tenth of July, we left Alexandria en route to Barcelona and Madrid. I travelled on my mother's Egyptian passport and we easily got an exit visa as she was Spanish-born and I was still underage. She was so excited about returning to Spain after more than nine years of absence that she couldn't sleep the night before our departure.

She spent most of it chatting with Dad and making sure he would be all right by himself, while he promised to join us in Madrid the following summer. They both agreed that if the political and economic situation in Egypt had improved in the interim, we were to return to Alexandria for five years more until I finished school. Back then what thrilled me was the prospect of a sea-trip and a long vacation.

Early in the morning, Dad took us to the harbour and we boarded the *Benicasim*, property of the same Shipping Company I was to use again on my definitive trip to Spain in 1964. Those ships carried agricultural products across the Mediterranean and Mom recognized the *Benicasim* as one of the fleet of four ships that regularly brought her olive oil.

The eight cabins on each of those ships limited the number of passengers to sixteen. People booked those informal cruises to relax, eat well and visit seaside cities. Some passengers were heading nowhere and embarked on a round trip just for the fun of it. Other vacationers took their cars aboard, disembarked in Italy, France or Spain, toured one or more European countries and returned to Egypt when their holidays were over.

A single fare cost thirty Egyptian Pounds (five euro), full board included, for a journey that could last up to two weeks. Tapas of ham, cheese, shrimp and wine were served on deck before lunch but those extras were charged to one's account and paid to the purser before the end of the journey. You never knew beforehand which ports of call the ship would definitely make, or how many days the trip would last. While cruising, the Captain could unexpectedly change his course to pick up freight from a non-scheduled dock.

We went ashore during the one or two day stopovers and visited Beirut, capital of Lebanon, which back in 1957 was a cosmopolitan, busy, noisy and multilingual city, still unspoiled by future political turmoil and wars. It was a lavish city, bursting with boutiques, restaurants, entertainment and the famous brothels in the red-light district. Beirut looked nothing like Egypt, whose economy was going down the drain and where imported goods, plentiful in the past, had vanished; Alexandria's empty shop-windows only bore witness to the shortages, displaying low-quality Egyptian manufactured wares.

By contrast, Beirut stores were packed with everything. We didn't have much money to spare for trifles but mother listened to my plea and bought me an Elvis Presley record and two miniature medieval lead knights, a starting point to the fine collections I have built up over the years.

Mom's devotion to sea and sand dragged us to Saint Michel beach, one of the finest in Beirut and comparable to the best shores in Alexandria. The ship was our base to which we returned to eat and sleep after our daily excursions.

The port of Latakia in Syria, our next stop, had no piers for ships to dock. We dropped anchor half a kilometre off-shore and large barges took turns to empty and reload the cargo in the holds. Using the wooden ladder hanging down the side, I jumped off into the sea and swam around the ship. My mother, who never learned to swim, stood on the deck, watching me. The next stopover was Marseille, and on the eleventh day we arrived at the Port of Barcelona where my aunt Marisa was waiting. We headed directly to the airport, caught a plane and landed one hour later in Madrid.

Madrid was at the end of July as hot as it could get; much hotter and drier than Alexandria and lacking its cooling sea breeze.

Marisa who used to always live in guest houses, had recently bought from a distant relative an eighty square meter apartment in the smart district of Moncloa, ten minutes' walking from downtown. She got it for a very good price as the relative, a bank teller was forced to leave Madrid when he was nailed for banking fraud; but he wasn't prosecuted or jailed; he was just sent into exile to the bank's minor branch in the Canary Islands. We found later that he has increased his monthly income by forging client's signatures on teller's cheques and cashing the money for himself. It became his evening hobby! As he had a family of five, the bank's directors felt sorry for him and were merciful: instead of firing and suing him, they banished him to the "fortunate islands"—which in those days were not so fortunate, renowned or wished-for but today are considered a "golden exile" for the lovers of sun, sea, desert, and year-round mild, boring climate. The man never returned to Madrid; he retired and died there.

In 1957, Spain was still in the grip of poverty. It hadn't yet recovered from the Civil War and Franco's dictatorship wasn't doing much to help. The country had been ostracized by democracies since the end of World War Two but this stalemate would soon end, as the tourist industry was about to knock on the door. Spain also opened a window to the outside world when President Eisenhower and Franco signed an agreement by which American military bases were to be established on Spanish territory.

Actually, at the height of the Cold War in the late fifties, the United States was desperately looking for trusted allies in South Western Europe. They couldn't count on France's General De Gaulle because of his anti-American sentiments or on Italy, as the Republic was under the thumb of the Communist party. Ironically, this situation left Spain which had been ostracised for its fascist regime and support for Germany during the war, as the only "European strategic friend" of the United States apart from the United Kingdom.

America needed an anti-Soviet ally and new military bases and Franco became the flavour of the month. The American administration thought they had found an unconditional "yes man"; but Franco was no "yes man" to anyone: he had proved it by keeping Spain isolated for almost twenty years. But he would gladly accept what the Americans were offering as long as they could provide the help he needed to raise the country from political and economic ashes and place it on the European map once more.

President Eisenhower visited Madrid to finalise and sign the binding agreement. Encouraged by propaganda the crowds received him as a saviour. Both heads of State were cheered on the main avenues of the capital when they rode in Franco's convertible Rolls Royce, a present from his old buddy, Adolf Hitler.

The lights in the offices and apartments of the then tallest building (the thirty-storey Torre de Madrid on Plaza de España) were artfully switched on in such a way that the letters "*IKE*" flashed from top to bottom of the facade. The multitude joyously yelled his name but pronounced it the Spanish way: "Eekay" "Eekay". Eisenhower asked Franco what they meant by "Eekay" as if the people of Madrid had mistakenly taken him for someone else.

My grandfather's prostate cancer was terminal. He was living in an old people's home but was soon transferred to his own home. In September he fell and broke a hip. The doctor and the priest arrived simultaneously at his bedside. The latter was more useful than the former who could do nothing as by early evening the old man was dead.

For a couple of days, I was relocated with relatives to spare me the experience of the burial and funeral which they thought was unfit and hurtful for a child. In those years, mourning was a very serious matter. For three months, my mother and aunt dressed in black from head to foot and wore no make-up at all. After the funeral, we took a "recovery" holiday in the Madrid Sierra and stayed in the same hotel prize-fighters used to train and rest before major combats. At the end of the month and before school started we returned to Madrid.

Shut up in the Madrid apartment, I missed the freedom I had enjoyed in Alexandria where I spent there most of my time outdoors, on the beach and in the street playing ball, or sitting on the back of a garden bench, feet planted where buttocks should be, talking to friends and neighbours walking their dogs and watching kites flying high on the wrong side of the track (the popular and populous Arab quarter of *Hadra,* one kilometre from home across *Abukir Avenue*).

People from my generation or the generation before remember well where they were and what they were doing when President John F. Kennedy was assassinated in Dallas on 22nd November, 1963. I vividly remember that on the day he was shot, twelve-thirty Dallas time, it was nine-thirty in the evening in Alexandria. I was sitting on a garden bench with my friend Adel who left for Canada four years later. It was dark and the only lighting came from the surrounding buildings. We were talking about the future; within months I would be leaving Egypt for good. Adel asked me about Spain, of which he knew very little, how it was there and what my plans were. He was worried about his future; although of Lebanese origin, he was about to be drafted for three years into the Egyptian army and couldn't find a way to get off the hook. Fortunately, he only served a few months and was released from duty as a new law was passed stating that Egyptians of foreign descent could not serve in the Armed Forces.

After the 1967 six-day war, he left for Canada and was to be the spearhead that opened the door for the rest of his family to follow later. That night we were totally unaware of what had happened until the following morning when we heard the news of Kennedy's assassination on the radio and read about it the newspapers.

But what I missed most in Madrid was a taste of the movies, the genuine article. All films were dubbed into Spanish by a handful of non-professional performers, mostly radio speakers, who lent their pompous, bland voices to everyone. American actors all sounded the same, from Humphrey Bogart to Gary Cooper; it was pathetic and unreal. Censorship and its infamous scissors was also everywhere, cutting innocent kisses here, changing "unsuitable" bits of dialogue there and forbidding most films to the under-sixteens. Even prudish American films of the fifties were not spared. In *Mogambo,* for example, Grace Kelly became her husband's sister to soften her adulterous relation with Clark Gable, who was having an affair with Ava Gardner.

Italian Neo-Realist films were welcomed, as the Regime wanted to show the Spanish public how poor and hopeless Republican Italy was in the hands of the prevailing Communist Party; a good example was the film *Miracle in Milan*, where the action takes place in a slum.

The French Nouvelle Vague was handled in a different way, i.e. it wasn't shown at all. France was also a Republic like Italy, but Franco admired President De Gaulle (shortly before he died *Le grand Charles* made a private visit to Franco in Madrid), a general like himself. He praised his strong rule and the determination which had saved France in the fifties from economic and political chaos. However, French Nouvelle Vague cinema looked suspicious and could be misinterpreted by Spaniards—who were in those days the carriers of "eternal values", leading them into dire straits while losing their soul in the process.

Until my grandfather's death, my aunt's boyfriend Julian—although an investor—had only played a small role as far as the foundry was concerned. My grandfather was running it with the help of my aunt. When he died she took over the business with the help of the staff. In late 1958, when we were back in Egypt and he had been fired from the Ministry of Commerce, Julian began to interfere, pulling strings and managing her interests.

I didn't like the Madrid Lycée Français. I was admitted there after a short examination to verify my level which was surely very poorly done as I got stuck in the same grade I had successfully passed months before in Alexandria—meaning that in the process of changing schools I had lost one year.

There were few native French teachers; most were Spaniards with a good knowledge of French. The students were a cocktail of bad-mannered, spoilt brats from Madrid high society and a minority of foreigners, the children of the French Diplomatic Corps and other Embassies stationed in the capital. Discipline was lax and some of the French kids were rude; they quarrelled and called each other names like *fils de pute*, (son of a whore), something unheard of in Alexandria. They spoke Spanish all the time, in and out of class, and if it were not for my French textbooks, I could have believed that I was in a Spanish school.

The French *Baccalauréat* and the *Bachillerato* were taught simultaneously for those students who would later chose to complete their studies at a Spanish University. Classes ran from nine to six, with a two-hour break between morning and afternoon tuition. At noon I took a bus home, ate lunch and rushed back to school. On Wednesday afternoons, we were taken by coach to the school's sports field on the outskirts of town, to exercise our talents in gymnastics and to practise other sports like football or ping-pong. The Lycée was later relocated to those sport-grounds where it stands today as part of an ever-expanding city. The old school in downtown Madrid became the French Institute.

Our teacher of English was a Spanish lady and as I was the only one able to speak the language with ease, we frequently engaged in endless conversations that kept the rest of the classroom speechless and in awe.

In February 1958, my cousin Fuad came to Madrid on business. He was by now a Major in the Egyptian army and the General Manager of a shipping company in Alexandria.

He brought along a colleague, a merchant ship officer called Captain Ebeid which mispronounced sounds like egg in Arabic. My aunt, who never missed a trick immediately baptised him "Captain Egg". We took them to Toledo and showed them round Madrid. Both men were over six feet tall and towered over the rest of the population. Fuad, pointing at two little soldiers not taller than five foot two, poorly dressed in shabby uniforms, jokingly asked if children in Spain were drafted into the army.

The average height of Spaniards is increasing but fifty years ago it was very usual for a man or a woman to be around five foot tall; my mother and aunt (beautiful as she was) were no taller than that.

"Captain Egg" fell for my aunt, hurriedly proposed marriage and immediately received his marching orders. Back home he was probably married with a bunch of kids. Maybe he wanted to take a second or third wife, which is absolutely legal according to Muslim Law if one can supply their needs and treat them all with respect.

But that good Captain was obsessed with Spanish women. A year later, on one of his trips across the seas, he met a girl in Barcelona. She was called Lola and owned with her brother a sailor's bar and cathouse called *Los Cuatro Aces* (The Four Aces) in the downtown "Barrio Chino" (red-light district).

She was twenty-five and a brunette with a milk-white skin, (he was more on the *café au lait* side), big breasts, meaty arms, large thighs and an arse like a small van—just the way he liked his women. The Captain, as all sailors do during stopovers, lingered at the Four Aces in the wee small hours of the morning, before closing time, drinking Coca-Cola or whatever he drank and calling her *batta*. He would then take her to bed, liked what he sampled and promised marriage if she would come to Alexandria for additional testing and to check again to see if the little brown chap was a perfect fit for Lola's piggy's bank slot.

She came in the summer of 1960 and sometimes—when she wasn't busy tending to "Captain Egg"—she accompanied us to the beach. She sat on a rock facing the sun displaying her large pale sexy thighs and hoping for a quick tan. My mother cheerfully welcomed her as she had finally found someone to talk Spanish to. Lola was a barfly but also an entrepreneur, she owned her place of work and that made her worthy of respect. Who knows what they told each other during those beach sessions. As the months passed and Lola's relationship with the Captain remained stagnant, with no marriage in sight, my mother probably discouraged her from that most dubious path, urging her to go home to take care of her cathouse, as she would be better off in her own familiar, charted territory.

One day Lola vanished without saying goodbye and we never saw her again. For some time we kept speculating on her whereabouts. We never knew if she was back in Barcelona minding her studs or still in the arms of the naughty Captain (very improbable) who was keeping her in a private harem for his exclusive use and enjoyment.

To put on some weight and develop some muscle on my very skinny frame, I had recently started to practise bodybuilding. Plentiful Lola almost ruined my health and my training sessions as each night in the privacy of my bedroom I started to practise wild sessions of a very different type, while concentrating on Lola's big thighs, but very especially on her large hairy, fat pussy I knew she kept hidden under her yellow swimsuit.

We also took Fuad and the Captain to a Flamenco show. Flamenco music is similar to Arab harmonies, filled with laments, sorrows, unrequited love and cunning unsolvable problems. Both men watched in awe at the eldest singer and dancer in the *Tablado* (flamenco group), a fat gypsy woman in her fifties they kept calling *hadja* (a *hadj* or a *hadja* is a Muslim man or woman who has travelled on a pilgrimage to Mecca, an action that commands respect and confers a better social status).

When the show ended they told her that she looked like the *Set* (lady) *Umm Kulthum,* the greatest singer in the Arab world. They further encouraged the whole *Tablado* to come to Alexandria where they would be a hit. Like good Muslims, they only drank soft drinks so alcohol played no part in their overstated enthusiasm. They finished their business in Madrid and returned to Egypt one week later.

I dislike sports in general and most particularly those focused on the "concentration of the masses". I am no "team man" but a loner and in my youth I only practised sports related to personal skills and effort such as bodybuilding, swimming, cycling and ping-pong.

This individualism and solitary drive proved very successful when at fifty, I started my "one-man business". After a professional life of non-stop frustrations, toiling as a brainless fool for bunches of useless idiots, most not even fit to shine my shoes; my maxim now is: No partners, no bosses and no employees. Why throw good, hard-earned money away on useless mind-wrecked troublemakers.

Entertainment for the crowds, such as football, baseball and American football is centred on bending and directing the foolish mob towards common objectives, whether economical, political or patriotic.

The easy prey is the stupid and the weak i.e. the "mediocre" Mr Nobody who accounts for the vast majority of the world's population (though I'm convinced that the balance is fair enough for societies to function), and whose numbers are hopelessly increasing thanks to the daily brainwashing by moronic television and radio programmes and strings of repetitive commercials targeting a torpid, compliant population.

I reckon however that, though the mentally harassing of the people is necessary, (this is no place to go deeper into this point as it's too long and controversial), it's shameful to link (as done during international football matches) the real values of a country to the exploits of twenty-two spoilt modern gladiators in short pants kicking a ball around.

I understand the mental limitations of Man in general and the followers of such sports in particular, yet I cannot fully understand that a team of eleven guys with no background and no bottom, who think with their feet and whose only ability is to artfully kick a football can draw the respect and the adulation of the masses.

This entertainment can be compared (as has been said) to the games of ancient Rome. However Rome had an edge: admission to the arena was free and bread—the lack of which frequently caused riots and unrest amongst the populace was thrown to the crowds, "courtesy of the current Emperor".

Our world looks more like a follow-up to ancient Rome than the outcome of the centuries of darkness after the fall of the Roman Empire, when Europe brought down by religious superstition, sank into the gloom of the middle ages.

The Romans had as we now do the same currency but not the same language (though English has almost but not quite become our Latin); they built roads, bridges, swimming pools, spas, shopping streets, provided sanitation, immigrants, apartment blocks, sexual freedom, graffiti, you name it!. Roman games were tougher and more pitiless and bloodier and more exciting and macho than any of the sports the masses are presently pushed into. Gladiators were stronger and braver than any of today's football players, who look like a bunch of faggots, only caring about their public image and the undeserved millions they so easily make.

Slavery was one of the dark sides of the Roman system but house slaves were kept fed and bedded in their master's houses which is more than today's "rubble" (not rabble) can say. The "rubble" is what I call the unemployed, who are and often unemployable for life. They start looking for a job become lazy, stop searching and end up living on welfare or charity or stealing or begging, though they have helped in building the society which has discarded them.

Shall we sink again into the dark ages? Are there any new and strong barbarians waiting at the gates? I hope so, as starting all over again is the only way to save man from his demise.

In the spring of 1958 my second cousin named José after his father, but whom we called Pepito, took me to a football match featuring Real Madrid and some other first-division team. Pepito, twelve years older than me, was the son of my mother's infamous step-uncle, who yearned for an affair with her during the Spanish Civil War.

Following his father's footsteps, Pepito was trying (but not very hard) to be a lawyer but at twenty-six, was still a student struggling for a degree with the help of the bribes his father regularly sprinkled on his examiners. He finally got his degree but never practiced law. As his father died soon after he graduated, he inherited a substantial sum of money and retired to a small estate he bought in the Valencia countryside from where he conducted some petty business just for the fun of it.

Pepito and his father were life-members of the Real Madrid Football Club. They paid an annual fee to be able to watch all the matches the team played at its home stadium, the Santiago Bernabeu.

That was my first (and last) match. The game was then different and funnier. It was less defensive and a lot of goals were scored, to the great delight of the spectators. I hardly knew the rules of the game but I enjoyed watching the "whites" (Real Madrid) at their best. In the fifties they were winning the European Cup year after year. The team was the pride and *enfant gâté* (spoilt brat) of the rejected Franco Regime which used the Real Madrid triumphs and worldwide fame to bargain for recognition. Football icons such as Di Stefano, Gento, Puskas and others were that day on the field playing at the top of their form in the open and classical style of the fifties.

In Cairo in the early sixties, while I was still in Egypt, Real Madrid, played a friendly game against an Egyptian team (the Zamalek I think) which they defeated fourteen to one. The Spanish team accepted the inflicted goal as the "honour goal" for the Egyptians.

As promised my father came to Madrid in July 1958. During our absence from Alexandria he had turned into a complete vegetarian. He didn't explain the reasons for this drastic decision and we didn't question him thoroughly as we knew he wouldn't give us a straight answer. My father when confronted with topics he wished to avoid adopted the exhausted attitude of a Christian martyr in the Roman circus about to be thrown to the beasts and sadly asked if we meant to insult him.

We suspected that the reasons for becoming a vegetarian had originated in some restaurant he must have attended while we were away. Maybe a fat juicy *sorsar* had found its way under his steak, or he had been dished up decaying meat at one time or another. He never told us the reasons that led to his decision.

My mother said nothing but thought that his newfound habit was just spoilt-child bullshit (she believed that my father, as the youngest in the family who didn't marry until he was forty, was a spoilt brat who had had an easy life), and now a pain in the arse, as she was compelled to find a way to feed him with meat proteins without arousing his suspicions. She managed to fool him a second time (the first was when she tried to get pregnant by piercing his prophylactics), by adding mincemeat to his soup and pasta. He sometimes detected them, calling them "strange little unidentified things" but Mother was quick on the uptake and convinced him that those suspicious aliens he saw floating on his soup were only tiny pieces of vegetables.

We had a family pow-wow to reconsider everyone's future. Mother would definitely return with Daddy to Alexandria and it was left for me to decide if I wanted to stay with my aunt and finish school in Madrid or if I chose to go back to Egypt. I didn't hesitate much and decided to return as I missed Alexandria, my freedom and my street life.

I was aware that since the 1956 October war Egypt was not and would never be the same and that the future would be bleak for Europeans and Egyptians alike. However, my friends, school and movies were there. I was also aware that I would leave Alexandria for good in five years' time after my graduation. Things couldn't get that bad in five years, I thought. I decided to give it a try and make the best of what was left there.

At the end of August we embarked again on the *Benicasim*, the same ship that had brought us to Spain the previous summer. Julian and Marisa took us to Barcelona in their brand-new Renault 4X4, which looked like a small version of the Volkswagen Beetle. The five of us piled up in a car designed to accommodate two standard adults or five midgets. The luggage was securely fastened to the roof-rack.

With the windows lowered (it was August) Julian did the driving, the talking, the bragging and the smoking, while trying not to burn his pants with the embers from his cigarettes, blown all over the car by the incoming wind. My father who sat next to him for leg room, kept silent. My aunt, my mother and I squeezed into the back seat; we were small people (almost midgets) and didn't feel too uncomfortable.

We left Madrid in the evening; the road to Barcelona was narrow, bumpy and crowded with trucks. It took us seventeen hours to cover the six-hundred and forty kilometres with an overnight stop in a Zaragoza inn, arriving at one o'clock in the morning and a lunch en route the following day.

I was flabbergasted when the waiter at the roadside restaurant where we had lunch addressed my father as *abuelo* (grandfather) as I had never thought of him from that angle. The man probably thought he was too old to be my father; though he was only fifty-six, he looked older than his age as people at that time aged quickly. Even today in Egypt, a man in his late twenties or early thirties may look forty or more. Is it the climate they endure, the food they eat, the rotten environment, everyday worries, the feeling of hopelessness, the sweeping corruption . . . ? Who knows?

My father and I stood two generations apart at a time when a man was old at sixty and life expectancy wasn't more than seventy.

We arrived in Barcelona in the evening. We headed towards the harbour to board the *Benicasim* scheduled to sail at midnight. A couple of cranes were busy loading thousands of sacks bound for the Middle-East. The Captain and the Officers were the same we had met the year before on our incoming journey; it was the end of the summer season and we were the only passengers on board. We kissed my aunt and Julian good-bye. Marisa promised to come to Alexandria in a couple of years, which she did. That night the *Benicasim* steamed out from the port of Barcelona and headed first to Marseille and then to Genoa. Early in September we docked in Alexandria.

CHAPTER FIFTEEN

Nothing seemed to have changed much in a year. While we were away, my father had moved to a new apartment just fifty metres from the old one on the other side of the garden.

The first film we watched on the day following our arrival was *Giant* at the Odeon. Afterwards, mother reckoned that it was good to be back: "Movies are better and more enjoyable than those shown in Spain" she said, as if to compensate for any unhappiness her return to Alexandria might have caused her.

I immediately re-encountered Yorgho the neighbourhood friend I had known since we made the move from the district of Victoria to Camp-César four years before.

He lived with his Greek aunt and her husband in a two-story building bordering our common garden. His mother was Greek and his father Lebanese but for reasons unknown to me he was left as a small child in the custody of his aunt. When he came of age he adopted Lebanese citizenship.

He attended a French religious school, Saint Vincent de Paul, but was no good with books. At fourteen, he dropped out and was hired as an apprentice in a mechanical repair-shop owned by a Greek called Nico (Nicholas) who was a specialist in the maintenance of the diesel pumps used by trucks. He took Yorgho under his wing, treated him like a son and taught him the trade.

Years later Nico left for Greece and Yorgho went into business. It was a joint Egyptian partnership venture, as a post-revolution law stipulated that a foreigner could only own forty-nine percent of any business hence the need for an Egyptian partner to front the rest. Yorgho still lives in Alexandria and is the best engineer in his field after he became a specialist in Mercedes engines. Truck drivers come to him for repairs, spare parts and advice from such faraway places as Luxor and Aswan.

Although he is an entrepreneur and his own man, at sixty-five he was forced by law into retirement and sold his shares to his Egyptian partner—who is now in trouble because he has no business experience and can't find anyone with Yorgho's know-how to replace him.

With its smooth lawn, scattered trees and a few benches here and there, the small public garden facing our homes became our playground and private domain. It was like an oasis sheltering our games and encounters. The place was well-kept, and watered daily by a town-hall gardener in black *Mamluk* (the *Mamluks* ruled Egypt before the Mohamed Ali dynasty and were originally slaves—*Mamluk* in Arabic means owned—from the Ottoman Empire; the word is also synonymous to Janissary) loose trousers and a tight, sleeveless jacket which was standard wear for gardeners. The trousers were so ballooned that the man could have shat inside them and still pass unnoticed (except for the smell, of course).

He took pride in his work and wouldn't tolerate destructive interferences with his precious lawn, which we used for wrestling contests and other games. He came after us each time he thought we were doing damage, walking towards us slowly but steadily, knowing that, like a flock of wild birds, we would fly away before he could reach us.

Once, instead of escaping like the rest of the boys, I foolishly stood my ground and challenged him. He caught up and slapped me with his hard calloused hand; but I reckoned that he had a sense of order and discipline rare amongst Egyptian lower classes. That day, through humiliation, I learned a lesson of civic responsibility that has served me forever.

Yorgho became my closest friend; I was always impatient to get back from school to resume our street recreations. Playing with marbles was one of our favourite games. Small marbles filled with bright colours were sold by the dozen in small plastic bags. Large ones called *acro* were decorated with attractive and bizarre motifs; sold by the piece they were more expensive and much more tempting than the small ones.

The kids queued up to win and *acro* by shooting at it with small marbles from a distance of four metres. If it was your *acro* that was in the line of fire and the shooters were lousy, you could make a fortune in small marbles before one good marksman hit your "big one" and took it away. Yorgho was the luckiest of us all. At the end of the day he proudly went home with his pants pockets looking like two saddlebags filled to the brim with small and large marbles.

At the end of September and before school started, I was assigned a teacher of mathematics, my nightmare subject. I was no good with maths whether for a lack of initial orientation or because my brain was incompetent with numbers. Our Madrid trip had put me behind schedule and had achieved nothing. I was again in Alexandria and my folks were worried that this new alteration could cost me another year.

I was really poor at maths, but good at history and geography, top of my class in English, very good in French, and not bad in Arabic. Nevertheless maths, geometry and physics were also important subjects that I badly needed if I wanted to progress successfully through my finishing years.

My other—moral—difficulty was that I was carefree and a bit lazy, an "absent minded shithead" as I think of myself not only in those days but well into my twenties. I didn't bother poring over books, did my homework double-quick and carelessly wasted most evenings playing in the street with my rascal friends. My mother never taught me discipline and the hard sacrifice studies require; she never worried about the future, leaving everything to fate and good luck. My father, who never contradicted her, seldom interfered with my life; he must have thought I was a lost cause, out of his reach and beyond redemption.

Except on the eve of examinations, I spent no more than one hour a day on my homework and yet, at the end of school terms, I was always "lucky" and passed my exams with average marks which allowed me to move on to upper grades.

In October 1958, when classes began, I was placed as expected one grade below the classmates I had left the year before and who, on the first day, thought I had chosen the wrong classroom and kept calling me to their ranks.

I got acquainted with my companions for the next five years who are still my friends, now scattered all over the world in Montreal, Paris, Rome, the United States and Australia. We keep in touch because as you get older, you plunge deeper and deeper into the seas of your lost youth.

Yorgho was and still is my best and most faithful friend and could have come to Spain if he had wished to. In 1964 when I left Egypt he was eager to leave Alexandria and come to Madrid. He was a good professional and could have worked, with a little help from my aunt and Julian who had contacts there, for Barreiros which was Spain's largest truck manufacturer.

But he lacked confidence daunted by new challenges away from the country he had never left. He chose instead to stay in Alexandria and did well there so it's all for the best. At the time Yorgho was dating a beautiful but unreliable Greek girl, a real bitch he was madly in love with but who was only after his money, played around with other guys and made his life miserable for ten years. Possibly this affair had something to do with his decision to stay in Alexandria.

The Lycée Français is located near the Chatby tram station which runs below street level and is accessible by a steep flight of stairs. The school was built on a site of approximately one hectare. On the south side of the building, across a narrow street, stand the sports facilities the size, of a football field.

Its construction began in October 1913 and was one of three Lyçées in Egypt (the two others were in Cairo) built by the French Government and the Mission Laïque Française, as a bastion and spearhead of French culture and civilisation. It's an impressive ochre edifice, standing on high ground, its colonnaded façade facing north to the sea, five hundred metres away.

On the other side of the street, stands the imposing domed structure of the Collège Saint Marc, the largest Catholic school in Alexandria. The Collège is run by French speaking friars and, aside from the Lycée, it provided the well-off with the best french education money could buy. The Frères accepted students from all creeds and never leaned on or influenced anyone's beliefs.

Each morning, we entered school through a narrow grey door on the east side of the building that the *bawab* closed at eight o'clock sharp after he had rung a small bell hanging from a wall inside the senior students playground for exactly fifteen seconds. If that bell jangled and you were still not close enough to beat the *bawab* to the school door . . ."that bell had surely tolled for thee". Late students had to go in through the main entrance and prepare themselves to confront the *censeur* (the censor) Mr Chevrier, whose son Jean-Pierre was in my class. A teacher of English, Mr Chévrier was also in charge of other matters such as discipline. Once inside the building, the tardy pupil would slink unchallenged along the main corridor past half-a-dozen offices. Then, just when it seemed that danger was left behind and least expected . . . . there he was, the hound Cerberus in the shape of Mr Chevrier silently standing round the corner guarding the gates to salvation, the playground and classrooms. If you were not too late and Mr Chevrier was in a good mood—rare but not impossible—you could get off the hook with a reprimand. Otherwise it was *une ou deux heures de retenue* (i.e. coming back to school in the evenings for one or two hours' detention and doing your homework there).

Before the events of the 1952 Revolution and the 1956 Suez War which changed Egypt forever, the teaching of religion in all Lyçées was banned. We received a secular education and never talked or discussed religion which was left to the privacy of each family. Parents looking for religious teaching had to go elsewhere and there were plenty of Jewish, Christian and Muslim schools. We received a modern and practical education: classical languages such as Latin and Greek were out and English and Arabic were in.

At five minutes to eight in the morning, we lined up in our classes in the playground, seniors and juniors alike with one teacher heading each. At the strike of the hour and as soon as the *bawab* had closed the side door, we marched to our classrooms in silence and in an orderly fashion one behind the other.

In the early sixties when Egyptian fanaticism was riding high and our school, which had been nationalised was no longer a Lycée Français but the Lycée Al Horreya, we all sang (while still in formation) *Allah Akbar,* the battle hymn of the Republic (of Egypt), meant to remind us of the forthcoming final combat with Israel.

When the bell rang again for ten o'clock break, we stampeded from our second-floor classroom, down the stairs to the toilets or the canteen. But, on the ground floor and looking up, there was Mr Bahout waiting for us.

Mr Bahout, the overseer was a tall and ramrod middle-aged Lebanese, who wore metal rimmed glasses and always dressed in black, from his shirt to his overalls. It was rumoured that he was rigid and dressed sombrely because he had lost his wife in tragic circumstances, but who knows what's in a man's mind.

He waited for us in the pit of the stairway, from where he could observe the three floors above him, watching our furious descent and shouting *touchez pas à la rampe* (don't touch the banister). It seemed like a useless and gratuitous exercise but it gave us a sense of discipline, self-confidence and physical balance. I haven't lost that habit: I never touch handrails on buses or in the tube and try to keep my balance swaying on both feet as the train moves; to open doors I use my knuckles, not my fingers. The thought that thousands of unclean hands have gripped those handrails gives me the creeps. I know that one of these days a sudden stop will possibly send me rocketing across the wagon onto the driver's lap but . . . . *Allah Akbar.*

Mr Bahout juggled with a large, heavy ring strung with dozens of keys which he threw with gusto at the heads or torsos of the boys who were running away from a deserved rebuke. He was also very good at maths and willing during breaks, to gratify us with a demonstration of his talent. We suspected that he had been a teacher in the past, maybe a "defrocked" one.

Saturday mornings took a different turn; it was the last day of the week when staff and students took it nice and easy. Our English teacher Mr Allen, a short, muscular fellow with a crew cut told us of his combat days with British marines during the Second World War. He was also a navy expert and explained the features of the different units, such as destroyers, battleships, carriers and submarines.

Our Arabic teacher, Mr Wafa, a very open minded fellow (the same one who dealt with the case of the French teacher's feet on the bench), indulged us for twenty minutes with a rock concert performed by a mate named Victor and myself. Victor was all Rock and Roll, while I was a crooner, a ballad singer. He always performed *Jailhouse Rock*—the only song he mastered. He started his act by marking the tempo with his knuckles on the blackboard behind him. He always comes to mind every time I listen to that classic song or watch the film. After his performance, I sang the latest Elvis slows: *Don't leave me now* and *You're so young and beautiful*. We both got our shares of cheers, applauses, hisses and boos.

For his age, Victor was quite a hirsute beast, with dense black hair covering his legs. We were intrigued and didn't believe him when he bragged that he had seen all those movies, forbidden to under-sixteens that we all craved to watch, until he told us "very hush-hush confidentially" of his little secret. He said that while handing his ticket to the usher and before he could be sent away, he quickly turned up his trouser-legs, to his bushy calves, and calmly asked the astonished man if it was likely that an underage boy could be so fluffy. He swaggered, claiming that this argument always prevailed.

Mr Gamil, our Egyptian teacher of French literature was a highly educated man with a diploma from the Sorbonne in Paris. He loved the French language and on Saturdays he took pride in reading aloud the best composition of the week. He read frequently one of my essays as I was one of the best students in French but no-one in the classroom cared to listen or pay any attention to him and as soon as he started to relish in the beauty and the richness of the language as expressed by one of his pupils, an awful brouhaha of conversation filled the classroom. He tried to obtain silence but soon gave-up, weary of so much incomprehension and ingratitude.

CHAPTER SIXTEEN

We were only sixteen or seventeen when we started our secondary education but were considered by the Regime as old enough to follow "school army training" which was another of those hare-brained ideas dreamed up by President Nasser and his team of morons to give us a pre-taste of the real draft which would fatefully befall us later. There was little doubt then that Nasser was concocting some nasty projects concerning the future of Israel and certainly planned to launch, sooner rather than later, some terrible onslaught against his sworn enemy. He thus wanted his schoolboys to be fit and ready for the "final battle".(Israel, which was being continuously harassed, smelled a rat, attacked first on 5th June, 1967, and wiped out that first day Egypt's entire air-force).

We trained in blue trousers, shirts and caps, specially designed for our new "corps" with black shoes and British army belts and leggings bought in the old souk; these were decrepit and colourless as if they had been used in World War Two North African campaign so I freshened-them up with a coat of white paint.

A young moustached lieutenant fresh from the Academy, neatly dressed in his brand-new uniform, wearing Italian sun glasses and accompanied by a thin army sergeant in fatigue overalls, came to school twice a week to initiate us into the joys of military life. For training purposes they brought one *Maüser* six-shooter rifle and a manual explaining all the things we should know about "closed order", the military exercises performed in closed spaces. By then there were only seven boys left in my class. The sergeant did his "drilling" by walking us up and down the playground in a make-believe mini-formation. Then we stood in a semi circle around the lieutenant who carefully took apart and put together his rifle showing and explaining its basic components. He said, as army men always do, that our weapon was our life insurance and reiterated the importance of keeping it clean and oiled at all times. He then read a couple of pages from his manual, asked a few questions and that was that.

He emphasized once that the *Maüser* was a very powerful rifle (and still is) which could shoot a bullet through seven fifty-litre drums filled with water, each one being placed three meters from the next. I was amazed with such fire power and thought that one bullet fired at a man standing first in a line of seven, could instantly pierce through all seven men if the bullet didn't encounter any hard bones during its trajectory.

Once a year, they took the whole school for target practice with live ammunition to some barracks along the *Corniche*, in the Rushdi district. There was a big gun there overlooking the sea, which reminded me later of the Turkish guns at Akaba from the film *Lawrence of Arabia*.

Its muzzle was covered with a hood to protect it from the humidity that rises very high all year round in Alexandria. I wondered how this solitary, rusty contraption from another age, securely anchored in cement and which had not been fired for years, could possibly protect the town from the designs of an invading modern fleet.

Three huge rounds of ammunition lay next to the gun ready to be loaded as soon as the enemy ships showed up but they were probably unusable as the powder must have been damp and over its "sell-by" date.

It was the first time I had fired a war rifle and the deafening noise of the bullets breaking the sound barrier was impressive. The modern *Maüser* is still used in wartime by snipers and by hunters to shoot big game on African safaris. The recoil was so brutal that it was more of a match for Hemingway's stocky shoulders than my skinny bony ones. We did our shooting lying on our bellies. To avoid unpleasant surprises I pulled the butt firmly against my shoulder, breathed deeply, took aim and, as instructed by the sergeant, slowly squeezed the trigger. We had six rounds of ammunition each and we shot at one of the man-sized targets planted fifty metres away at the foot of a thick red brick wall punctured from top to bottom with bullet holes.

Albert, who was in a different grade, confessed that after experiencing the reality of live fire he felt that, should he go to war someday, he wouldn't come out of it alive. I kidded him and replied that nobody comes out of life alive.

The candid part of this "school army training" outlining the ingenuousness of Nasser's regime in spite of its fierce appearance, is that our Jewish classmates—who were supposed to be the enemy—were also trained with the rest of us. It looked as if Egypt was willing to provide its foe with basic military knowledge which could turn against itself if those Jews migrated later to Israel, as some of them did.

The Egyptians could never figure out Jews. Some aggressive posters depicted them as strong, pitiless and bloodthirsty beasts, armed with knives and guns going on the rampage, killing women and children; others were quite the opposite picturing them as submissive, harmless and vulnerable bearded old men dressed in black and leaning on a cane.

I wondered what the officials in charge of State propaganda were thinking when they designed those posters. They probably believed that the large, beastly Jews they had never met were holocaust survivors newly arrived in Israel from Eastern Europe. By contrast the compliant ones could very well be Egypt's mild Sephardic Jews whom they knew so well and who had lived peacefully amongst them for many generations. "Beware of them all" seemed to be the message as they can come to you in many disguises. The candor of the Egyptian people is touching and endearing and one must love them the more for that.

My aunt Marisa visited Alexandria twice more, in the summers of 1960 and 1963, when she brought from Madrid the first transistor pocket radio we had ever seen. She liked to laugh and mildly criticise the natives whom she thought were a little slow to react. She was used to the sparkling mind of the *madrileños* who are quick on the uptake.

She considered Ibrahim our *makwagi* (the ironer), in his late twenties whom we affectionately called *Hema* a handsome man with his moustache and looks of actor Omar Sharif. But it's as commonplace amongst Egyptians to look like Omar, as some Welshmen may look like Richard Burton. Ibrahim rented one of the two shops on the ground floor of our building. The other was taken by two young Coptic brothers bearing biblical names I can't remember; they sold candy and cold drinks and took turns in minding the store open twelve hours a day.

The *makwagi* was indispensable. The laundry was washed at home but good and cheap pressing was Ibrahim's business. He heated his heavy irons on a Primus petrol stove and tested their temperature by holding them near to his right cheek, which bore a wide scar, the result of being too close for comfort. If the iron was too hot he plunged it for an instant into a water-filled tin basin he kept beside him on the floor. He then ran the three kilo appliance over the garment laid on his ironing board, an archaic wooden table covered with a thin white cloth. His hand holding the iron moved swiftly and skilfully up and down the clothes, which had been previously mouth-sprayed with the exact quantity of water a neat pressing requires. The inventors of the electrical steam-iron surely owe much to the Egyptian *makwagis*, pioneers in the art of ironing and who probably learned it from the *khawagat*.

He charged one piaster (one hundredth of an Egyptian Pound) for a shirt and two piaster for a pair of trousers. To us these amounts are so small: they are impossible to understand as they only represent a percentage of a cent of a euro. His rates included same day pick-up and presto delivery with a smile, clothes neatly pressed and folded. Years after I left Alexandria, Yorgho told me that Ibrahim has been in and out of jail for hashish smoking, a common practice indulged in by many men.

Hashish is used to achieve happiness and well-being just like Prozac or any other medication modern shrinks prescribe. The authorities are aware of it and are lenient with the smokers but not with the dealers especially the small ones.

On my last trip to Alexandria in November 2010, I asked the limo driver, a copt (to calm Western tourists he had fixed a cross and an image of Christ on his dashboard as if these symbols separated the good guys from the bad) who took me from Cairo to Alexandria, where the very new Egyptian riches came from. He reckoned that great fortunes of over one hundred million dollars came from hashish trafficking on a massive scale. I guess Ibrahim was unlucky to get caught, or maybe he had started dealing to make some extra cash. He died at sixty but not of a drug related disease.

Hashish can be smoked in cigarettes, (a joint) or mixed with apple—or strawberry—flavoured tobacco called *measal* (honey-like), using the Arab water-pipe called *sheesha.*

Smoking the *sheesha* is a ceremony only carried out in Arab cafés or at home. The limo driver also told me that the advantage of the *sheesha* over cigarettes is that you had to go looking for the *sheesha* while cigarettes came after you. By that he meant that you can smoke cigarettes everywhere and all day long (continuously inhaling nicotine and tar) while the *sheesha* can only be enjoyed in certain places after working hours to soothe one's nerves and banish daily stress.

To increase their earnings some small-time dealers mix hashish with tiny pieces of dried dark shit as both colours match perfectly. There is no reek of excrement as dried dung has little odour; besides the smell of hashish is so strong that it obliterates any other. Hashish is sold as a small piece of dark-brown paste, wrapped in a piece of paper.

Men smoked hashish on Thursday nights, their ears glued to the radio to hear the glorious sound of Umm Kulthum, the greatest female singer in the Arab world. These weekly concerts were the culmination and perfect ending to a chicken and rice dinner finished off with tea and sweets often more than an average diabetic could stand (Egyptians have a sweet tooth and diabetes is very common).

Umm Kalthum sang for hours on end till well past midnight. When she picked up an inspiring word or a lavish sentence, she didn't let go and repeatedly sang and re-sang it using different tones and modulations making each song last up to half-an-hour. *Habibi* (my love) is a theme word in most Arab songs and she constantly reiterated it with ups and downs of joy and sadness that her privileged, tireless voice allowed. She was a fat woman and held a large, embroidered hanky that she used to wipe-off the perspiration from her forehead, cheeks and neck.

Men sat by their radios, their bellies filled with goodies, their lungs saturated with smoke, slowly sinking into a stupefied torpor, probably dreaming that they were dead and had gone to heaven, or that heaven had magically crept inside their bodies through mouths, nostrils and arse-holes.

I am a very musical man (in the good sense of the word as musical also means faggot) but I am unable, for good or bad, to appreciate or judge the value of Arabic music so different from our own tempo. However, *Umm Kalthum* or the *Set* as she was called out of respect was surely a very talented singer, able to secure the adulation of the Arab masses for many decades.

Habibi is very frequently used in conversations and means also "my friend" or "my dear one". My aunt Marisa who, during her trips to Egypt learned a few Arabic words, called the Egyptians *habibis*; "How are my *habibis* today?" she jokingly asked me; "Are they *kuayes*" (fine). She had a happy nature, a good sense of humour and enjoyed life the more for it.

My mother, who hated Arabic music because of its pitches and slow monotony of the melodies and the lyrics which she couldn't understand and cracked her nerves, renamed the great lady of the Middle-East *Umm calzones*. The word *Umm* in Arabic means mother and *Kulthum* sounds like *calzones* which is an old Castilian word meaning pants; thus the musical idol of the Arabs became at home the "mother of the trousers".

Over the years, I had acquired a set of boring, little habits, a repetitive routine that my aunt quickly picked up to make fun of me. Whenever she had the chance, she pulled my leg by gleefully reciting "*Odeon, Gaité, clo-clo, Délices*". The first two items were the neighbourhood cinemas I assiduously frequented; the *clo-clo* was the chocolate, ice-cream cornet I bought during intermissions and *Délices* was the downtown pastry-shop which I haunted for my favourite cakes.

One of our regular sports played in the street with the *makwagi* and the boys from the candy shop was a game of skill and strength consisting in breaking a three-centimetre in diameter sugar-cane (firmly held at both ends) with a single karate chop. Ibrahim sold the one-meter sticks which he also displayed at the front of his shop to attract customers. He who broke the cane with one blow of the hand would twist and chew the hard and fibrous texture to suck the sweet juice, while the loser paid for it and watched.

I never listened to my mother who warned me of the dangers of excessive sugar and that senseless forced exercise, plus the other hard candy I regularly ate, put a terrible strain on my teeth. Decay soon set in, marking the beginning of a long costly, painful and boring love-hate affair with all sorts of dentists.

Friday is a holiday for Muslims as Saturday is for Jews and Sunday for Christians. This arrangement was carefully planned by the gods to prevent any of these religions stepping on the other on their day of rest.

The Arab calendar has only names for Friday and Saturday. The other five days are numbered, from Monday, "the second day" to Thursday, "the fifth day" (Sunday is thus considered the first day of week)

Portugal, unlike Spain, doesn't take much interest in its Arab heritage as the relics from the Arab conquest are not as evident there as they are in this country. However, the Portuguese calendar is a copy of the Arab one. Saturday and Sunday are the only days of the week with a name; Monday is also called *segunda feira*—second holiday following Sunday which is obviously the first—and so on till Friday which is called the *sexta feira* (sixth holiday). It would seem that everyday is a holiday in Portugal (which happens to mean "orange" in Arabic). I don't know if these are the only two languages with no names for certain days of the week. The popular Portuguese *fado* with its rich Arab nuances deep Arab connotations is a counterpart to Spanish Flamenco and the south of Portugal, the Algarve, translates into Arabic as *al guarb,* meaning west as this area is located on the Atlantic facing America.

Another one of my "civilised" and "innocent" games was to shoot little birds with an air rifle. Two different models were available on the market. The first, shooting larger pellets, was called "number one"; it was meant for the big boys and designed to hunt large prey such as pigeons and crows. The second type, which I owned, was known as "number two". It shot smaller pellets sold in boxes of five hundred and was the perfect weapon for shooting sparrows and small birds without blowing them apart.

The rifle was loaded by "breaking" it in the middle, allowing the spring to activate the pump that would compress the air into the chamber. A pellet was then inserted and the gun was ready for action. You could carry that "harmless toy" freely, anywhere and use it in the open. I often fired it indoors too during warm summer nights, to kill flying *sorsar* strolling on my bedroom ceiling.

Those rifles were better and shot farther than the classic American bee-bee gun but they didn't have the advantage of the latter's repetition system.

Whenever I checked the firing power by shooting point blank at the hard pavement, the pellet smashed onto it and spread out into a very thin film of shining lead with a fringe round the edges. If I shot at the softer street asphalt, melting under the burning sun, the pellet would puncture it and disappear.

I could bring down a little bird from a distance of ten to twenty metres, a good performance considering the limited power of the weapon. I roamed the gardens and parks, searching for understanding little birdies willing to keep still while I aimed and shot; moreover the countryside was not far from home. Yorgho and I went there from time to time, more for the fun of it, a sense of adventure and a feeling of isolation than for the pleasure of hunting.

We crossed open fields, risking unfriendly encounters with *fellaheen* who could have come after us with sticks and stones to happily break our bones in trying to protect what they thought were their endangered women and *gamoosa*—not necessarily in that order—from the dangerous presence of the young *khawagat*.

However, the best hunting ground was the sports field of the English Boys' School renamed Al Nasr (victory) school. I stood outside the enclosure and shot at the birds on the grass: there were dozens of them pecking and hopping around. I didn't choose a target but shot at random into the bulk, hoping for the best. When I had a hit, I jumped the railings, which was hazardous, because I was then exposed to the looks of the pupils who were using the playground or—worse—to the hawkish eyes of the caretakers always on the lookout for trespassers. I once shot a bird but when I picked it up wasn't dead but badly hurt. I didn't know how to end its agony and tried to drown it in a puddle. Killing the bird in that way was for me a brutal and terrible shock. The poor thing refused to die quickly as I had hoped; to the end it kept stretching its thin, wet neck, quickly opening and closing its beak trying to grab some air; it was a horrible, unforgettable experience. That same day I threw away my rifle and since then I have never harmed any living creature large or small—except for the *sorsar,* of course.

CHAPTER SEVENTEEN

The Shaker—family or the tribe as I called it—comprised eight members including five boys and a girl. They were of Lebanese descent and lived in my neighbourhood on the ground floor of a white building with a small garage in the backyard.

Well into his fifties, the father of the family Joseph Shaker was a teacher at the Lycée Français. He was small and thin and pale and looked as if he were about to die on you any minute. He was a chain smoker and often displayed a hard predisposition, both probably due to the unbearable load of many offspring and a small income. When I compared his salary to that of my father, who was also a teacher, I wondered how that family could make ends meet.

The boys went to the Lycée and the girl, the youngest, to a convent school. I knew them all well, but I made friends with Chawky who was my age. He had been my classmate for two years but being no book cracker, he was transferred at sixteen to the school's trade section which granted those who didn't wish to continue their education further than high school a commercial diploma enabling them to get a regular job or start in business.

But Chawky was most happy and in his element when he played the bongos which he had bought in a second-hand shop. He chose drummer Gene Krupa as his idol and model and learned to play them at home (my home!!) to the great distress of my mother who thought with each bang that she was hearing the menacing tam-tam death messages from the dreaded Mau-Mau in the dark continent.

His efforts (and our patience) paid off and he finally did well in the music business. Very soon and—till he left Alexandria in 1968—he was playing the drums (real ones) and singing professionally at *Santa Lucia*. This was a famous, exclusive restaurant and night-club located downtown in *Safia Zaghloul* street, where most of the city's cinemas and restaurants were to be found.

The family owned a 1920 black car slung high on its wheels, like the ones used by American gangsters during the Prohibition. I used to call it later as Elliot Ness's car because when the father and some of the boys jammed inside it and drove away, they looked like "the untouchables" on their way to raid a speakeasy or a bootlegger's warehouse.

Chawky was the first in the family to drive it. He had no licence but in Egypt that was unimportant as there was no traffic violation that a small *baksheesh* to the right *shaweesh* wouldn't cure. Like most vehicles in Egypt then and now, the car wasn't insured: the large number of accidents meant that policies are much too expensive and besides, Insurance Companies are thought unreliable and regarded by car-owners as scoundrels who won't protect their customers or foot the bills. Whenever there's an accident, drivers often choose to settle matters, big or small, between themselves.

In any case, Chawky's motor-vehicle was not a public danger; it couldn't have hit sixty kilometres per hour even if their lives had depended on it. Moreover Chawky was a good driver, heavy traffic was inexistent and the chances of a mishap were not very likely. He once (but never again) let me drive his obsolete, four-wheel jalopy (which would cost a fortune today as a vintage car), into their parking slot at the rear of their house. I almost wrecked it as I kept revving it mercilessly stepping on the gas pedal while holding down the clutch with my left foot. Alarmed by the protests of the senile engine his father came to the window shouting like a madman and cursing hell in different languages. It was sheer luck that with such an uproar I kept my cool and didn't abruptly release the clutch which would have sent the vehicle crashing into the garage's back wall.

To increase his monthly income, Mr Shaker gave private evening lessons for which the old vehicle served its purpose well. He was driven to his student's home and back by one of his boys who waited patiently on the street, smoking cigarettes and teasing girls passing by. Worn-out and shaky, I'm sure Mr Shaker wouldn't have lasted one round in the hustle and bustle of public transportation. Besides, the *Ramleh* trams running inland and the buses dashing along the *Corniche* to the beaches and the Royal Palace of *Montazah,* were not always the best way to reach his many and varied destinations.

The standard Egyptian fire cracker is a small ball the size of a marble, made of gun—powder mixed with tiny yellow stones, wrapped in brown paper and secured with a thin wire. We called them "bombs" and they could, if misused, be dangerous causing damage to hands and face. They were sold in dozen bags and when tossed at neighbourhood buildings, they exploded with the sound of a pistol shot, and left indelible black marks on the façades. We were always lucky and got away with it as no neighbour ever complained of those dark spots on the white walls.

Chawky turned up one day with a "brilliant" idea saying that it would be thrilling to build a really large explosive, a homemade "bomb" to end all "bombs". He wanted to check out the devastating effect of dozens of those small shells exploding in a single blast. He had probably read somewhere or watched a film about Hiroshima and Nagasaki and wanted to witness first-hand the results of a nuclear explosion, as halfwit tourists did from Las Vegas, when nuclear devices were tested in the Nevada desert in the fifties.

I only hoped that he wouldn't try to smash his "big one" onto a neighbourhood building as, this time the damage would be too obvious to pass unnoticed. We built our device sitting on the stairs of the landing outside my apartment. We had bought four dozen standard "bombs" which we handled with great care, separating the wrapping from the powder, which we kept in a glass. We then joined the short wires together to obtain a long one and finally we poured the forty-eight shots of powder into a piece of newspaper, rolled it all into a compact ball and tied up the whole thing.

And then . . . . all hell broke loose. Chawky was still handling the bundle and I was one metre away, when the contraption blew up to his face. The walls seemed to crumble down on us and the noise was so deafening that Chawky lost his hearing. Terrified neighbours came out of their homes thinking World War Three had started (it was during the Cuban missile crisis). Fortunately, no-one was hurt and Chawky got off with temporary deafness and some light bruises on his face. The lesson served us well; from that day, we stuck to our small and much safer gadgets and never again tried to repeat such a perilous experiment.

Following Nasser's aspirations of Pan-Arabism, an agreement was signed with Syria in 1958. Both countries came together to form the United Arab Republic: one-two star flag and two "loving" people joined for better or for worse. (Syria had been an Egyptian province in the very distant past).

Nasser's idea was to create a "United States of Arabia", adding more and more stars to his banner, as other countries joined. This giant Arab state would then wage war on Israel. The Nazi scientists he brought to Egypt toiled long and hard to build the middle-range earth-to-earth missiles he hoped would knock out his sworn enemy from the face of the region. It is not clear how many missiles he thought were needed to achieve his goal but, all in all, there were only six rockets which were occasionally paraded on the streets of Cairo during revolution celebrations and which looked as if they were made of stuff from a Hollywood B war movie. The feat of erasing Israel from the map cardboard was the first step towards his crowning as the indisputable Arab Führer and liberator of the Palestinian people, a modern Saladin or a recycled-macho-Lawrence-of-Arabia-minus-the-camels. Unfortunately for him, no other Arab country joined his exclusive, fearful Club and the brief union with Syria was dissolved in 1961.

A couple of years after this pact had been signed, Field Marshal Amer, Nasser's right-hand man was dispatched to Syria as Governor there and watchdog of what Egypt thought of as its newly-acquired rich Province in the Levant. To humiliate the Syrian administration and to teach them how to rule their own country for the greatest benefit of Egypt, the Marshal brought to Damascus a cohort of Egyptian civil servants to occupy top positions in the Syrian administration.

No union between Arabs is possible because of political and ideological discrepancies. Divergent backgrounds and tribal loyalties make them quarrelsome, mistrustful and elated. They mistrust the *franga*, their former colonisers as much they had despised their Turkish oppressors for hundreds of years. They suspect and reject alien-decadent-infidel-customs and way of life, which they at times adopt for their own convenience abroad (or at home) but which, they conveniently refuse to contemplate when they contradict their strict religious upbringing and other deep-seated local habits.

For Arab states, democracy is and will always be an impossibility considering the people's strong sense of individuality, their idiosyncrasies, and the high rate of poverty in many of the countries as well as the rampant, historical and everlasting corruption.

Fifty years ago when Egypt had in President Nasser a potential unifying leader, a massive, unrestricted, coordinated Arab strike, supported by Russia's weaponry could have wiped out Israel. But Arab leaders were too corrupt and coy to carry out any extreme action which could have damaged their standing and interests with the rest of world. Hence, Israel who understands its neighbours better than they do themselves can rest assured forever because of the Arab lack of unity and sense of purpose. All wars past and future between these two people so similar (as far as middle-Eastern Jews are concerned) but divided by history are just unimportant clashes meant to alleviate regional tensions or to serve world interests.

As expected, the Syrians took the Egyptian meddling in their affairs very badly. After all, they are a proud breed, strict, harsh, a no-nonsense people and drinkers of *arak* (a sort of *eau de vie*) which makes them courageous and bold. They are in a way the descendents of the fierce anti-Crusaders, heirs to the Phoenicians and their roots go back to ancient Mesopotamia, one of the oldest civilisations in the world.

Egyptians are quite the opposite. They are the most open-minded, gentle people in the Middle East, the offspring of innumerable cultures (some European), who for thousands of years swept the country from end to end. They are kind-hearted and carefree with a fine sense of humour.

So in 1961, when divorce came because their policies were incompatible, the Syrians also proved that they not only had the guts to kick the Egyptians out, but also a good sense of fun. Before putting Field Marshall Amer and all his cronies on a plane to Egypt, the Syrians shaved half of the ex-Governor's moustache; there were no razors aboard so he could shave the other half and avoid the disgrace of coming home to Cairo half the man he was when he left.

In the Arab world, a fine moustache is considered a symbol and source of pride, of manhood, authority and respect. It separates men from boys and machos from faggots. Men often risk their moustaches in bets they are always sure to win, and are filled with shame when they lose and off goes their sexy attribute, for everyone to see.

Years later, Marshall Amer was made responsible for the Egyptian defeat in the June 1967 six-day war with Israel and was murdered at home—probably by Nasser's inner circle—delighted by a cold, sweet, delicious—and poisoned—*gawafa* (guava) juice.

At twenty-one Egyptians are drafted into the army for a period of three years with the exception of only children who are exempted. It's a merciful, practical law. Elder sons have to provide for the women and younger children should the father and head of the family fall ill or die; neither is it fair that the only male child of the family should be killed in a war, depriving the household of an heir. I think that my exoneration from service was crucial for me. I don't know how I would have taken it or what I would have done if I had been forced to serve for three years in an army filled with *fellaheen* and the prole.

The ironic twist to this episode was that at twenty-one, I became a Spanish citizen, and was therefore called up into the Spanish army. In Spain, no-one was excluded from National Service and all men from nineteen to thirty-nine were called to arms; this duty applied to everyone: gimps, midgets, idiots, half-wits, delinquents, flat-footed, the myopic, the illiterate and psychopaths included.

To get off the hook amongst the certificates I submitted in Madrid to the military authorities proving that one year before I had been discharged from soldiering in my former country of Egypt, was the translation into Spanish of exonerating Arabic documents that had been validated by the Spanish Consulate in Alexandria and which my parents—for safety reasons—sent by diplomatic bag.

But all our efforts were to no avail and in January 1967 I was drafted into Franco's army. The fourteen months I served were not all bad. After a three-month drill on the outskirts of town, I was appointed to the Ministry of Defence in Madrid and spent most nights at home. Three months before the end of my term, I became a lance-corporal and was assigned to the military police headquarters where I had an easier life. Sometimes I think that by not re-enlisting and becoming a sergeant at twenty-five and slowly rising through the ranks to become a lieutenant at sixty, I may have I missed a quiet "brilliant" career.

In Alexandria, Chawky (who was my age) was also called up—with four brothers there was no way he could make believe that he was an only child. One of his older brothers, Adel, was already in the ranks but was hoping for a quick way out before his three-year period was up. He was betting his release on an anticipated Egyptian law stating that all citizens who could prove they were of foreign descent were exempted from service. On weekends he came home from the barracks dressed in a shabby khaki uniform even uglier and more badly fitting than the one I wore later in the Spanish army and which made me look like a defeated Turk on the run in the film *Lawrence of Arabia*.

Early one morning Chawky, accompanied by his protective father, and dragging his feet left to meet the draft-board in the same old barracks we used for target practice. While they were walking, getting closer and closer to the army building, Chawky who is a good Christian, (a common occurrence in countries where minorities have to stick together) and a true believer, (which is rarer) asked for a miracle. Just like that, he ordered a miracle that would release him from service, in the same way I ordered a *fool* sandwich at my favourite joint. Once inside the barracks, they waited patiently in line getting closer and closer to a wretched table loaded with files and located in a small room at the end of a long corridor. Behind the table, a chain-smoking veteran and disillusioned Captain who had probably risen from the ranks, was signing up the constant flow of young blood which would very soon become cannon fodder as worthless as used toothpicks.

When their turn came, the draft Captain immediately recognised Mr Shaker as his son's teacher at the Lycée. This unexpected encounter restored hope. They confided in the officer asking if he knew about the new exoneration law for Egyptians with foreign origins. The Captain lowered his voice to a whisper and told them that the law would be effective in less than a month. He thus urged Chawky to disappear and especially to stay away from home, as his absence at the draft-board would be noticed, and he would be tracked down as a deserter. As far as he (the Captain) was concerned Chawky had never visited the barracks that day. That officer was a good man and he endangered himself and what remained of his career for bestowing such counsel.

Chawky left for Cairo, stayed there for a while, and returned to Alexandria when the Law had been passed and things had cooled down. He got his exoneration and his brother Adel was also soon released from his term. His miracle was accomplished; sometimes it pays to believe.

CHAPTER EIGHTEEN

In the early sixties, to reduce or at least stabilize the birth-rate which is the most dangerous scourge Egypt is facing, President Nasser came up with one of his few good ideas, a utopian and impractical project but that was worthy a try. He distributed to the *fellaheen* and the lower classes (who are reputed to think with their balls), as many free *kaput* (condoms) as they could use—which were many.

Those people, especially the *fellaheen*, normally take more than one wife (four's the legal limit) and breed extremely large families of a dozen children or more. It seems that Egypt is now close to having a population of eighty-five million (from the twenty-nine million it had when I left in 1964), though a true census is unfeasible as peasants don't declare some of their male children to spare them from National Service and keep them working in the fields.

They were intrigued by those prophylactics that had suddenly rained down on them but which they never used because no-one had bothered to give them indispensable practical lessons. Anyway they thought their dicks were too large and powerful (sometimes true) to fit into any standard contraption (different sizes were not available then); they also believed that fucking their women with condoms was like sucking a lollipop without removing the cellophane wrapper. Moreover they felt blessed and very comfortable with the string of children Allah was constantly sending them.

They never considered what they could do for their country because the country had never done anything for them. So they gave the condoms away to the village kids who blew them up and tried to sell them as balloons. Unlike today, there was not an inexhaustible variety of sizes and flashy colours (black are for mourning widows) to choose from. Sales were probably very poor as those fake balloons, although very tough, were small and pale with a suspicious tip on top that made them look like faulty, discarded stuff from a toy factory on the decline.

The girl Joy Akel became my joy during my last months in Alexandria. She was an only child and lived with her widowed mother a few blocks from my home on the first floor of a two-storey building bordering our crescent-shaped garden.

They were Palestinians and stateless and, like other foreigners in similar circumstances, they held a residence card issued by the Egyptian authorities allowing them to live in Egypt as refugees. She attended the Sacred Heart School that provided its students with a fine British education. She had sad, myopic grey eyes concealed behind rimmed spectacles and a cute well-shaped little body with good legs, firm buttocks and apple-shaped tits, which became the more attractive as she grew up.

For a few years, (yes, years) I watched her comings and goings from my room window on the third floor until she finally metamorphosed from a shapeless, thin teen ager into a sassy young woman. I was very shy and never dared to approach her but, encouraged by Yorgho, I took courage and finally at nineteen, I talked to her. In Alexandria, each foreign community kept "more or less" to itself and going out with girls, just for the fun of it, was not a common practice. You had to be formally engaged or at least prove your good intentions to take a girl out; her parents insisted on knowing whom she was dating. Is that boy's family well-off? What's his religion? What is he studying? Those were the questions they would ask. Money was a very important issue as women didn't work and yet expected to live like princesses from the Arabian nights. Boys were most protective of their young sisters and could challenge you to a fight if they knew or suspected that unobtrusively you were dating them.

I started to catch Joy's eye and ears by playing my Elvis and Sinatra records, the loudspeaker of my Philips record-player perched on the edge of my window facing her green shuttered balcony which I had been so eagerly watching for such a long time. Then one day we coincided on her doorway and that was that.

I took her to downtown cinemas (the expensive ones) a couple of times and we watched at the Rialto *Lovers must learn*. On our way home she asked if I'd learned something. At nineteen, I was still quite naïve and had not yet kissed a girl. She also knew that I would be leaving shortly for Spain and was no doubt smart enough to know that it was a very unpractical long shot to pin her hopes on me.

Sometimes in the evenings she invited me upstairs. On those occasions, I never met her mother who would retire to her bedroom as soon as she heard the door bell ringing. We dimmed all the lights and we sat on the couch. We kissed and I clumsily massaged her hard tiny tits, while she sighed and awkwardly reached for my cock. I tried to slide my hand inside her knickers but most of the time they were off limits; she pushed away my arm saying that the ways of Egypt were different from those of Spain as if she or I knew (but I discovered soon enough), what sex in Spain was like. I don't know if she drank regularly or only before my calls, but her mouth and breath exuded a sweet smell of anisette. Maybe mother and daughter felt lonely and needed a speedball. Eventually however, she stopped refusing a touch of my inexperienced pussy finger which couldn't tell the difference between clit and lips. On those occasions she turned so horny that she quickly climaxed while I pressed her against my chest. Panting, she rolled up her eyes and tried to satisfy me too by ruthlessly rubbing my wild and inexperienced dick.

It was a good thing that when I left Alexandria, I wasn't in love with anyone as the pain of leaving her indefinitely behind (as it happened later to Chawky) would have been unbearable.

For Joy as well as for the rest of us the world we knew was falling apart as life in Egypt was becoming daily, more unfamiliar and unpleasant. But where could those two women go? They were Palestinians and Palestine had disappeared and if it hadn't, it would be another part of Arab world in which their European culture and mentality wouldn't fit. They had no place to return to and because of their stateless condition no country would easily take them.

Joy was young, smart, lovely and well-educated. She could have made it elsewhere like we all did and though she had a mother in tow, they could have emigrated to the United States or Canada. But maybe they thought it was a hard step to make, a leap of faith. Instead, Joy chose the easy way out and married a wealthy Libyan.

In the early eighties I was working for the American Express Travel Services in Madrid and was visiting the Gulf countries to promote Spanish destinations amongst travellers from that area. On my way and before proceeding to Saudi Arabia, I made a three-day stopover in Cairo, to call on my friends at our Offices there and visit Yorgho in Alexandria.

While we walked the streets of our neighbourhood, I asked him what had become of my little Joy. He told me that, four years after I left Alexandria, she had married the Libyan citizen, lived in Tripoli, had two children and now . . . . they were all dead.

As I looked at him incredulously, he added that on one of their regular road trips from Libya to visit her mother and spend their summer holidays, they had had a fatal head-on collision with a truck on the last leg of the desert road from Al Alamein to Alexandria. The whole family was killed instantly, the only survivor being the children's poodle which was spared by taking refuge on the floor between the front and back seats.

As we passed her home I noticed that the balcony's green shutters were closed. It seems that shortly after the accident her mother went insane; she locked herself in the apartment and never came out again or spoke to anyone. The *bawab* and the neighbours did her errands until she finally died two years later.

In Egypt, driving is dangerous as many drivers don't obey regulations; walking is even more hazardous as there are hardly any traffic lights and fewer zebra crossings, always ignored by automobiles and traffic agents alike. Pedestrians have to take their lives in their hands each time they cross a busy avenue, dodging cars and flapping their arms about like dolphins to slow down or stop oncoming traffic, which amazingly . . . . obliges; the streets look like a *corrida* when the bullfighter swings his red and gilded *capote* to cut short the bull's initial charges.

Traffic is also hazardous on the Nile Delta route from Cairo to Alexandria called the agricultural road. It's one of the most populated regions in Egypt, crowded with fellaheen and livestock, who cross the motorway whenever it suits them best.

The other alternative, the eight-lane highway called the "desert motorway" is the most important and safest artery linking the two largest cities in Egypt with populations totalling more than thirty million. Though traffic is hectic and people drive as they please, oblivious of the "highway code", the chances of hitting a stray Bedouin on his camel are very slight indeed.

This reminds me that, while I was still in Egypt, one of Yorgho's customers driving the desert road at night (it then had only two lanes) ran down a camel which was standing still in the middle of the right-hand lane; His large Volvo crisscrossed between the legs of the animal, tearing its belly apart. The windscreen broke under the impact and man and car interior were heavily bespattered with guts and shit. He quickly drove away as he feared that the vengeful owner, probably a wandering Bedouin, would appear from nowhere and also tear his insides out to get even.

The beach cabins of the most privileged resorts such as San-Stefano, Stanley and Sidi-Bishr, were lined up at the back, below the promenade. These constructions were property of the Town Hall and rented by the year to those beach-lovers who were looking for a foothold on the sea-front to relish the many hours they spent there during the long summer months in comfort. They were painted blue and white, measured ten to twelve square metres and were used to leave street clothes, stock umbrellas and beach chairs, hang wet towels and swimming trunks to dry, eat in privacy the picnic basket brought from home, or in the heat of the day, enjoy a siesta, alone or accompanied on the uncomfortable narrow bed covered with a thin and shabby mattress.

The cabins I sometimes visited were ill-kept and reeked with humidity; a daunting odour of rancid food overwhelmed the sea smell. I felt uncomfortable each time I stepped in and the grains of sand scattered on the floor scratched my naked feet.

They were made of wood and metal and were regularly ravaged by the devastating dampness; in the winter they were repaired and repainted by the tenants, as it was their duty to keep the properties in good condition. The iron locks that secured the doors frequently corroded so when the cabin was not in use they were wrapped in a piece of oily cloth, which was soon also covered with rust stains.

On the beaches, tanned young men wearing tiny, tight swimming trunks and bearing Greek, Armenian and Levant surnames, looked for steady romances or one-night stands with the adulterous, middle-aged house-wives, who relaxed by their cabins or lay on the burning sand, under multicoloured umbrellas, reading magazines, encouraging their libido by sipping large glasses of cold peppermint, while their bald, fat bellied and indifferent cuckolded husbands stood by the shore, with their feet in the water talking business and mistresses.

The young studs captured the women's admiration playing tough games of beach tennis. Although the men were fully concentrated on their game and never looked their way, they knew well enough that the eyes of those sex-starved bitches were upon them, twinkling and shining like tiny clits. The players therefore tried to enhance their performance turning those matches into a gladiatorial contest, a brutal display of muscle, flexibility, skill and sweat to impress even further the horny females, who, like Roman matrons, wished for nothing better than to lay a handsome slave for one night in the privacy of their cabins, or in some discreet downtown hotel.

Those bloodless duels looked like a human version of the alpha-male animal combats, shown in the National Geographic documentaries, where male opponents fight savagely and relentlessly, intermingling and breaking horns, until one of the two, totally exhausted, relinquishes the coveted female.

Nevertheless and in this very different scenario, the only ones who could cross horns were the understanding husbands who stood on the seashore, their feet constantly bathed and refreshed by incoming waves and were probably not much interested in their wives' extra-marital affairs as those gave them lee way to proceed with their own indiscretions.

I liked that game of strength and precision played with narrow wooden rackets, tennis balls and straight powerful shots, the ball never touching the sand. It wasn't easy to strike at the speeding, sometimes wet, incoming ball and to send it back in the right direction. It required powerful wrists and stout forearms which I still didn't have.

During the summer months lifeguards were on duty from early morning till sunset. They had thin muscular brown legs, wore black T shirts and white trunks, and carried shrill whistles they used with no restraint to pull the swimmers out when the sea became rough.

For that purpose, a flag pole was also well-positioned in the middle of the beach. When the sea was calm, the pole was flagless and we could all hit the water and swim freely. A red flag was flown when the sea was choppy and foamy: bathers had to stay close to the shore and not venture into deep waters. Finally a black flag meant that the sea was extremely turbulent and that strong underwater currents made swimming dangerous even for intrepid swimmers who could be dragged straight out to sea with no chance of fighting their way back.

In spite of those warnings, there were always fearless fools to defy the odds; those were usually very good swimmers who liked to take their chances and challenge the sea in an unlawful and unequal duel. The crowd then stood on the shore anxiously watching a head in the distance, like a black dot bobbing across the frothy tips of the waves, while the lifeguard ran up and down the beach like a mad pelican, ordering the brainless bather to come back by jumping high, swinging his arms and whistling his lungs out.

The only way to survive that ordeal was to avoid exhaustion and drowning by just staying afloat without fighting back and drifting. Hours later the currents would finally spit the swimmer—dead or alive—onto another beach many kilometres away. At times, the tide would throw up onto our beach, the drowned corpse of some foolhardy fellow who didn't make it. The crowds would gather round with morbid curiosity, to see the bloated belly, distorted features and the swollen tongue shooting out of his mouth in a farcical gesture, till the police finally arrived, summarily dispersed them and the ambulance took the body away.

Flying kites is a popular entertainment in warm, windy climates; we flew ours all year round. Our launching terrain was the open ground facing home which was also used as a wasteland. Our standard design was made of three pieces of one-metre rods, tied together in such a way as to form a hexagon. The simple frame was held together with a string joining its six points and secured into small nicks in the rods.

The skeleton was then ready to receive the cellophane paper, which could be a monotonous one-colour sheet, or a lively kaleidoscopic of small multicoloured squares or triangles which we glued together. The homemade glue we used was a perfectly calibrated mixture of flour and water. The tail of the kite, four of five times its size, was also made of small strings of cellophane tied to a thread.

To fly them up to the skies, we used hundreds of metres of thin, white cotton string called *parachol*. To improve its resistance we ran the fibre through a ball of wax we held in our hand, while the kite was taking flight. The string had to be light because as the kite reached a height of one hundred metres or more, a heavy cord could bow and bring it down if the wind wasn't strong enough.

The *nahas* (copper) was how the man who cleaned copper utensils was called. It was also the name of a notorious and corrupt prime-minister during King Farouk's reign. Our more modest *nahas* performed his daily activities on the same plot of land on which we flew our kites. He cleaned sauce and stew-pans of all shapes and sizes that the neighbours brought to his place of work. To cook their food, Egyptians preferred copper to any other metal. It's a good heat transmitter and the food is cooked better as the temperature is evenly spread throughout the recipient: yet copper has to be polished regularly as it becomes a very dangerous poison as soon as a thin green film sets in.

The *nahas* used ordinary sand from the waste-ground to clean by hand the outer and inner surfaces of the pans scratching them until they shone like new pennies: the sand was wet and smelly and stained with human and animal piss as strollers also used the place as a public toilet.

Giant turds of all colours and shapes as big as houses and pointing to the sky scattered all over the wasteland, were constantly invaded by dozens of humming, green-winged flies, which at times, took a break from their lunch, and for a change of taste, hurried to lick the sweet lips of a kid enjoying a piece of candy nearby. These flies were real gourmets and knew how to switch, in the middle of their meal, from sour to sweet.

Once, while I was flying my kite, a man lifted his *galabiya*, and squatted for a pee a few metres from where I was standing. His dick covered with bumps (probably the result of venereal diseases), was so large that it almost touched the ground; when he had finished he picked up a stone and dried it by banging it a couple of times with the same strength and determination needed to strike two pebbles together.

CHAPTER NINETEEN

On 7th April, 1961, CIA trained forces and Cuban exiles tried to land at the Bay of Pigs to regain control of the country and topple Castro. Nasser fiercely rose in defence of Cuba and cursed the "imperialist" methods of the United States, whose financial help he had once requested to rebuild his country, but which Washington denied as the Eisenhower administration was convinced that he was nothing but a "red hood" under orders from Moscow.

In his desire to defend the weak, he presented Castro with a token of his moral support and organised a huge, "spontaneous" pro-Cuban demonstration in the streets of Cairo and Alexandria to show dear Fidel that the Egyptian people (who had never heard of Cuba), cared and supported his young revolution. To start such a march, the government used students as a spearhead. We couldn't refuse to participate since we were deep into pre-military training and though we hadn't sworn yet any allegiance to army or country the authorities could however wreck our lives by expelling us from school.

The demonstration was set for 9th April at ten in the morning. The day before, our lieutenant briefed us on the purpose of the march and said that he and the sergeant would be heading the parade. He also told us that the most important thing to attract the masses was to shout Castro, Castro, incessantly, at the top of our voices.

We totalled a hundred boys from senior classes, plus four or five hundred from other schools and we very much doubted that this display of support would become the successful demonstration our "dear" Raïs had promised Castro and his people. But we were wrong. At nine-thirty, we left the Lycée and slowly marched towards Ramleh tram station two kilometres away. Half-an-hour later, a rabble dressed in pants and *galabiya* joined in. One hour later, as we reached the central streets of town, there were thousands, stretching hundreds of metres behind, shouting Castro . . . . Castro. That's when my friends and I decided to call it a day; we inconspicuously slipped away from the multitude and went home after kindling the flame of a massive demonstration, which was described the following day by all the newspapers, as one step further in the fight against imperialism. Sometimes big things have small beginnings.

My grades at school were very average. I wasn't spending the necessary time on my homework or paying full attention during classes. In the evenings I was impatient to finish what I had to do and join my friends who were waiting in the street good and ready for me.

My parents were very tolerant with my poor results and mildly rebuked me when I brought home my monthly marks, which were often beyond the pale. I was good with languages and the pet of our English teacher Mrs Apostolides, but I was average or below average in everything else.

My mother didn't care much; she only believed in luck and fate. My father told me in an even but authoritative voice that if I didn't stop playing around and start caring more for my studies, my already predictable graduation marks (of approximately fifty percent) would be insufficient to enter any Egyptian college—which required average grades of sixty-five percent. But his remarks left me cold. Years ago, it had been decided that as soon as I finished High School, I was bound again—this time on a one—way ticket—to Madrid.

My Italian friend Livio, also an only son, was the opposite; the only thing that brought us together was our love for music. At school, he was top of the class in every subject except Arabic. He had joined us from the Collège Saint Marc when the learning of Arabic language became compulsory for all, regardless of nationalities, thinking that the Lycée would be more lenient. That requirement was not a school's decision but decreed by the Ministry of Education and applied to all foreign schools in a nationalistic attempt to inculcate the new-found importance of a language which had been despised and neglected for centuries.

Livio, although born in Alexandria from Italian parents whose ancestors came to Egypt generations ago, was not fluent in Arabic and couldn't have cared less, because as soon as he got his *baccalauréat* he would also be on his way to an Italian University. However, he gave it a try for one year, but again failed the end of the term examination. Finally his parents, putting a strain on the family finances, decided to send him to a French institute in Beirut for two years where he finished High school before leaving for Italy. Before Livio left us, our French teacher of literature encouraged him by saying that he was such a brilliant student that this "Arabic situation" was of no importance to him or to his future.

Livio was outstanding and very intelligent; the "little genius" as I called him was the epitome of tidiness and he took pride in perfection. He owned a Parker 21 fountain pen, which he filled, not from the ink pots placed on every bench where we dipped our pens and weekly filled by the *farrash* (caretaker), but from a small bottle of Parker ink he kept in his satchel. He used a set of pencils, the colours of the rainbow, and rulers of different sizes to enhance his exercises and presentations which were always impeccable.

But the reason that we made friends was obviously not our classroom affinities but our common passion for music and the proximity of our homes less than a hundred metres apart. In the evenings I often went to his place for some music and singing and never annoyed him by requesting his help with my homework. He was a composer and played the piano violently as if he had something to prove. He said that composers frequently played their instruments wrathfully so as to prove their creative talent and negate the futile efforts of performers. At times, his father, who was an employee in a foreign bank, sometimes joined us and played his violin. Before the Second World War, he was a professional musician and had played part-time in Alexandria's belle époque Grand Cafés and *Salons de Thé.*

When the Second World War broke out, the British rounded up all male Italians in Egypt (including Livio's father) and sent them for the duration of the conflict to internment camps just in case they grew too fond of *El Duce,* who had promised his people he would ride a white horse victoriously through the streets of Cairo.

I joined father and son in their music repertoire and sang melodies from the French *nouvelle vague* and Elvis's immortal slows. His mother, a very unobtrusive and sweet lady, listened quietly to our performances, frowning at the frenetic banging of her son on the piano keys. After we had finished, she mildly rebuked him:" Livio", she said "Why don't you play the way Cherry (my pet name) sings, softy and with deep emotion". He bluntly replied that most composers play their instrument with rage because they like to compose, not to perform, and thus become angry and aggressive when they have to play. It was an interesting theory and the final argument that always shut his mother up.

During the two years he spent in Beirut completing his secondary education, Livio returned home for the summer holidays and he once brought me the latest Sinatra album *I remember Tommy*, unavailable in Egypt.

Our last musical performance took place five years ago in the home of my French friends Bernard and Nadine. I hadn't seen Livio for more than forty years until we finally met up in Paris. He had been living most of his life in Rome and, like me, he was a self-employed entrepreneur on his way to retirement. He is a small man but I found him thinner than ever, weighing fifty five-kilos; probably his exceptional brain is still sucking-up his calories and physical energy.

He played on Bernard's piano, while I sang *My Way*. As soon as we had finished, Bernard begged him to stop: his style hadn't change after all these years and he was still playing too loud for comfort. Bernard was worried that his neighbours might start knocking on the walls; therefore we all went for dinner and safety.

In June 1963, we passed our final examinations: school days were over. Two weeks later, the results came out. In the school hall, my classmates and I waited impatiently for the *farrash* who would soon pin up the list of the fortunate who had passed. We stood there making sure that we were not dreaming by reading our names on the board over and over again.

But summer holidays were still ahead and I intended to make the most of it. I realised that I would probably never again see my friends. Livio had left for Italy and Platon, Chawky, Robert and Yorgho, would soon become shadows of the past. It was many years and lots of water under the bridge until I met them once more.

Those students who had passed their examinations with top marks could choose the career of their choice. Robert started medicine to follow a beautiful classmate whom he fancied, although he knew his love was impossible, he being a Jewish and she a Muslim. Others who had received average marks but wished to continue their education in an Egyptian University would have to settle for a less coveted career like history or law or give the *baccalauréat* another try the following year to achieve better results.

I never imagined that forty years later I would meet some of my pals, in Montreal, Paris and Rome. Our Egyptian classmates remained in Alexandria and pursued their education there. After graduation, some of them, desperate at not finding a steady position or a well remunerated job in Egypt, left for the United States and Canada as young graduates there were very successful and appreciated to their full value.

The remaining foreigners amongst them, "the last of the Egyptian Jews"—including my friend Robert—still refused to realise that they were doomed, and firmly hung onto a State that hated them, with a glimmer of hope for a change in government policies and a more tolerant future. Unfortunately they were finally expelled from the country in the aftermath of the June 1967 six-day war. Those Jews were the last leaves of autumn, still dangling from a winter tree. Like their predecessors years before, they scattered all over the world, in search of a new life.

CHAPTER TWENTY

On the day we passed our final examinations, only a very few students from my early years were still my classmates. Most of them had been left behind repeating lower grades while others had fled the country during the political events of the fifties. In the last three years there only seven boys left but we received a reinforcement of fourteen sassy broads from the girl's section to complete a full class of twenty-one.

In the summer of graduation year 1963, my aunt Marisa came to Alexandria for the last time. I was due to leave for Spain as soon as I got my exit-visa which was not approved for another ten months. Meanwhile my mother and she started to plan my future.

Marisa thought that I should study Economic Sciences, a booming new career with great expectations, but it required a good knowledge of mathematics which I didn't have; so they settled for Law School, a very honourable profession requiring a good memory to learn by heart a lot of useless crap. My aunt stated that smart conservative Spaniards settled for Law, as it is common knowledge that a lawyer can steal more money with a small briefcase than a bandit with a big gun. I had a good memory but unfortunately for her I wasn't smart or conservative or Spanish.

My mother didn't say much as she knew me well and was anticipating that I would never be a lawyer. She also wanted to leave Egypt for good and was possibly considering the angle that her sister owned a productive little business and that one day, as her only heir, I would take the helm of the ship, thus cementing my future and hers.

How little we knew at the time that four years later, Julian, my aunt's lifelong sweetheart, would sell her smooth-running business and run away with the proceeds and that the following year in Madrid, I would drop out from Law School (after a brief attendance of only three months), to follow the uncertain, fantasist course of a job in American movies, at the time being shot by the dozens in Spain. This Hollywood dream of mine took me on a road to nowhere for three years, first as a wretched extra and later as an interpreter of English in production departments, a feeble and unimportant link between the Spanish and the American crews.

My last summer in Alexandria was happy and light-hearted. I had no prospects for my immediate future and the obsession that was eating me up was to leave the country as soon as possible. I believe that the best way to enjoy a vacation is between jobs or in the middle of two different situations. One has shed the old worries and responsibilities and the new ones are unknown and yet to come.

My aunt returned to Madrid in September and sent me the work contract that was essential to get me my exit-visa, which finally came through in April the following year, after months of nerve-racking paperwork with the Egyptian authorities.

Meanwhile in Alexandria, I saw my future mostly misty and dim, sometimes filled with hope but often drowned in distress as I knew that my dreams were imaginative but unreal. I longed to be an actor and a singer but I believed I was not photogenic enough and that the camera wouldn't love me. I have a perfect musical ear and a good speaking voice but I disliked the quality of my singing voice, which I found dull and impersonal.

I was not a composer (a major credit in the sixties), didn't play an instrument and subconsciously knew that Spain was not the right place for me to start. Moreover to succeed in show business one must be lacking in a "certain morality" and also be street—wise which I was not. With such overwhelming handicaps, no wonder I never made it.

During the winter of 1965, my first in Madrid, I wrote two short thrillers. One was based on a true story I read in the papers about a failed attempt by the Egyptian Embassy in Rome to kidnap—and have him sent back to Cairo to be tried and hanged—, an Egyptian double agent who also spied for Israel. The man was caught, drugged, tied up and put in a trunk, to be part of diplomatic baggage. However, at Fiumicino airport, before boarding the aircraft, the operation aborted, as the wretched man woke up, started to scream and rock the trunk. The incident was a worldwide scandal and the Egyptians had quite a lot of problems weathering the storm. The other story I wrote was about a secret missile base in the middle of the Libyan wilderness. I found those stories so short and childish and abominable, that I instantly threw them away and gave up my career as a novelist.

By my actions, I was dictating fate which says that everything is written, only true because of one's limitations which are genetically implanted by generations of successful or hapless forebears. The unexpected, also to be occasionally considered, adds to and beautifully balances the equation of life.

I wonder why I didn't face reality. Was it because I found daily solace in a comfortable but precarious cocoon, which transformed my impossible dreams into a remote, but hopeful, possibility?

During my last winter months in Alexandria, Yorgho, Robert and I met a young streetwalker. She was twenty, married since the age of sixteen, slim, pretty and always wore the same shabby green dress. She made ends meet by ministering to the young, faithful European clientele she picked up at all times of the day in the garden of my neighbourhood inhabited by Greeks, Italians and Armenians.

Yorgho found her one afternoon, sitting on one of our benches and wisely negotiated rates and conditions for the three of us. Robert, then a student of medicine joined us craving for some practical anatomy lessons and a taste of fresh pussy.

Robert and I were not close friends during our school years, but our ties tightened when we each went our way. Moreover, he was an indispensable pawn in this operation: his parents had a rented villa near the Sidi-Bishr beach, at the far end of the Corniche, which we had free access to in the winter as they only used it during summer months.

We got there by tram and bus and walked in front while the girl, in her green dress and nylon stockings, followed a few metres back, as we would have been embarrassed to be seen in her company. We paid her one Egyptian pound each (fifteen cents of a euro) which was then good money considering that my father was earning only fifty pounds a month. Two of us sat on the terrace enjoying the soft sun, while the third fucked her in the master bedroom. We kept a lookout for police cars as we had been told that patrols were frequent, watching and protecting the area which was deserted in winter time. We were also informed that if we were caught with a prostitute, punishment could be severe for all parties involved. Nothing of the sort ever happened; we never encountered a policeman and no-one ever disturbed us.

We were almost twenty and still virgin. The first time I went in first. The girl was sweet with a young, well-shaped body and a neat, shaven pussy. A few minutes later and after a quick performance I came out slightly disgusted, maybe because I had been expecting something different. I threw my used condom in the toilet and told my friends that the whole thing was a little bit revolting and not as great as I thought it would be. Half-an-hour later and after both my friends had taken their turn, my "disgust" had vanished and a craving was back, stronger than before. I rushed into the bedroom again for a second round of hostilities which turned out much more profitable than the first one. My friends followed suit and in the end there were six bloated condoms floating in the toilet, refusing to get flushed away and making Robert nuts as he thought his parents would find them, if they dropped in for an unexpected visit. In the evening, feeling relaxed, happy and manly we celebrated the event by going to a downtown cinema.

At the end of March, and after a one-day trip to Cairo with my father to settle some papers in some Ministry, I was notified that my exit-visa had been approved and that I could drop in anytime I wished and pick up my travel documents.

On the following day when we went to the passport office, the precious visa stamped on my passport had been over-stamped with the word "cancelled". This meant that my visa had been first granted, then for no apparent reason, denied. We dashed for help to my cousin Fuad's office, only five minutes away. He was a coronel and the General Manager of an Egyptian shipping company. Fuad listened carefully to our grievance, took a look at my passport and asked his secretary to put him through to the Bureau. Though I couldn't hear or clearly understand the whole conversation, the harsh tone of his deep voice and his facial expressions made it clear that he was knocking the shit out of some low-rank officer. He then hung up the phone, told us that the whole thing had been a misunderstanding and that my visa was now ready and waiting. We thanked him and rushed off. Half an hour later, I had a brand new visa stamped on my passport and that day my cousin Fuad became my all time hero.

The next morning we went to the shipping company offices to buy my passage. The *Benidorm* wasn't due in Alexandria until 12th April, departing for Spain two days later. I still had to wait for another two weeks and was afraid that in the meantime some shadowy officer or civil servant might change his mind and re-cancel my exit-visa.

My father told me that according to regulations I could not take personal belongings such as my record player, records, books or collection of tin soldiers with me, but he was misinformed as often happens in Egypt. What the Law expressly forbade, in order to hurt the departing rich *khawagat* by depriving them of their possessions, was removing expensive furniture, carpets, jewellery, stamp collections, and other valuable objects from the country.

Ignorant of that fact, I hurriedly sold my tin soldiers and bought two pairs of shoes. I gave Yorgho my racing bicycle and some of my records. My other items I left at home hoping some day my mother would bring them to me. Good riddance I thought. That's the best way to start a new life. Father went to his bank and bought twenty US dollars, the only cash I was allowed to take out as travelling expenses.

I boarded the ship on 14th April, 1964 and felt relieved as if I had already landed in Spain. My parents left me well-installed on board and left. At sundown, the ship sailed east towards the Beirut stop over. I stood on the deck. I was the only passenger. The sea was slightly rough, grey and foamy and it had started to rain. I cried when I heard on the Captain's radio Charles Trenet's song *La Mer* . . . . dancing and dancing and swinging and rocking along gulfs and shores . . . . the sea is like a love song . . . . a love song under the rain.

Standing there on that deck and about to face a new life in a country I never really understood, I should have thought that I was soon to become a nowhere man trapped in a labyrinth of too many cultures. It seems that harbouring more than one can lead a man to insanity, but I prefer Scott Fitzgerald's intelligent and illuminating quote, which I have slightly modified "An artist is a person who can hold two opposing ideas in mind at the same time and still retain the ability to function".

The thin Alexandria coastline vanished behind the mist. I dried the tears from my eyes, returned to my cabin, washed my hands and went to the Officer's Mess to meet the crew at the dinner table.

I was almost twenty years old.

Madrid, June 2011
RICARDO WAHBY TAPIA